HOW TO READ THE HUMAN AURA AND CREATE AN INTELLIGENT LIFE FORM

DRAGONSTAR'S OCCULT SCIENCE SERIES

How To Read The Human Aura

And

Create An Intelligent Life Form

By

Dragonstar and William Walker Atkinson

Inner Light/Global Communications

How To Read The Human Aura And Create An Intelligent Life Form

By Dragonstar and William Walker Atkinson
Copyright © 2015- by Timothy G Beckley
dba Inner Light - Global Communications
All Rights Reserved

Printed in the United States of America

Inner Light/Global Communications, P.O. Box 753,
New Brunswick, NJ 08903

No part of this book may be reproduced, stored in retrieval system or transmitted in any form by any means, electronic, mechanical, photocopying, recording or otherwise without the express permission of the publisher.

Please address any questions about this book to:
mrufo8@hotmail.com

Timothy Green Beckley: Editorial Director
Carol Ann Rodriguez: Publishers Assistant
Tim R. Swartz: Editor
Sean Casteel: Associate Editor
William Kern: Associate Editor

Cover Graphics: © Deosum |
Dreamstime.com

For Free Subscription to The Conspiracy Journal Write:
Tim Beckley/Global Communications
Box 753, New Brunswick, NJ 08903
www.ConspiracyJournal.Com

How To Read The Human Aura And Create An Intelligent Life Form

CONTENTS

THE BEGINNING - Thoughts Made Real 7

1. WHAT IS THE HUMAN AURA? 17
2. THE PRANA-AURA 24
3. THE ASTRAL COLORS 29
4. THE ASTRAL COLORS (Continued)................34
5. THE AURIC KALEIDOSCOPE 40
6. THOUGHT FORMS 46
7. PSYCHIC INFLUENCE OF COLORS 60
8. AURIC MAGNETISM 65
9. DEVELOPING THE AURA 70
10. THE PROTECTIVE AURA 75
11. COLOR VIBRATIONS 81
12. THE MATRIX OF THOUGHT FORMS 106
13. THE FINAL STEP OF VISUALIZATION 128

How To Read The Human Aura And Create An Intelligent Life Form

THE BEGINNING

Thoughts Made Real

SINCE we are all part of creation, we also have the ability to be creators ourselves. This process can be observed everyday with the things we have built...our houses, cars, electronics. But it is not just the physical things that are part of our creations; our thoughts give life to our world, our reality.

One fascinating part of our ability to participate in creation is our ability to create living thoughtforms, or as they are known in occult literature, Tulpas. Tulpas are sentient beings imagined into existence using meditation-style exercises. People who create Tulpas are called "Tuplamancers."

The term Tulpa began known in the West in 1929 following the publication of ***Magic and Mystery in Tibet*** by the Belgian-French explorer Alexandra David-Néel. She notes that some Tulpas are created on purpose either by a lengthy process resembling the visualization of Yidam, or, in the case of proficient adepts, instantaneously or almost instantaneously. In other cases, apparently the author of the phenomenon generates it unconsciously, and is not even in the least aware of the apparition being seen by others.

How To Read The Human Aura And Create An Intelligent Life Form

"A Tibetan painter, a fervent worshipper of the wrathful deities, who took a peculiar delight in drawing their terrible forms, came one afternoon to pay me a visit. I noticed behind him the somewhat nebulous shape of one of the fantastic beings which often appeared in his paintings.

"I made a startled gesture and the astonished artist took a few steps towards me, asking what was the matter. I noticed that the phantom did not follow him, and quickly thrusting my visitor aside, I walked to the apparition with one arm stretched in front of me. My hand reached the foggy form. I felt as if touching a soft object whose substance gave way under the slight push, and the vision vanished.

"Even though the painter had not seen the phantom, he confessed that he had been performing a dubthab rite during the last few weeks, calling on the deity whose form I had dimly perceived, and that very day he had worked the whole morning on a painting of the same deity. In fact, the Tibetan's thoughts were entirely concentrated on the deity whose help he wished to secure for a rather mischievous undertaking."

A Yidam is a type of deity associated with tantric or Vajrayana Buddhism said to be manifestations of Buddhahood or enlightened mind. During personal meditation (sadhana) practice, the yogi identifies their own form, attributes and mind with those of a yidam for the purpose of transformation. Yidam is sometimes translated by the terms "meditational deity" or "tutelary deity." Examples of yidams include the meditation deities Chakrasamvara, Kalachakra, Hevajra, Yamantaka, and Vajrayogini, all of whom have a distinctive iconography, mandala, mantra, rites of invocation and practice.

The creation of a phantom Yidam has two different objects. The higher one consists in teaching the disciples that there are no gods or demons other than those which his mind creates. The second aim, less enlightened, is to provide oneself with a powerful means of protection.

Reflecting on this, a Tulpa is a sentient being that becomes incarnate, or embodied through thoughtform. A thoughtform is a small packet of condensed psychic energy and like all energy, the thoughtform can be programmed to carry out specific tasks and/or directed to travel to a target area. They are more than just fleeting flights of subjectivity that pass through our minds and are gone…they are our creations.

Thoughtforms are dependent on the people who generate the mental energy empowering them. A weak thought form will quickly dissipate, accomplishing nothing. Good or bad, they are expressions of human creativity.

The practice of creating Tulpas is considered to be extremely dangerous for anyone who has not reached a high mental and spiritual degree of enlightenment and is not fully aware of the nature of the psychic forces at work in the process.

Powerful thoughtforms, when neglected can wreak havoc. Energy feeds on energy and a thought form that is several weeks old will have absorbed all kinds of different influences, emotions and energies from its surroundings. This might appear amusing to some, but the mutated thought form has often been known to reappear in the locale of its creator, only to wreak havoc, due to the outside energies it has accumulated.

If there is one thing that is important to know, it is that every thought, even the most insignificant, is a living reality. On the physical plane, a thought is invisible and intangible, but it is no less real, in its own region and with its own subtle matter, it is a living, active being.

How To Read The Human Aura And Create An Intelligent Life Form

Once the Tulpa is endowed with enough vitality to be capable of playing the part of a real being, it tends to free itself from its maker's control. This, say Tibetan occultists, happens nearly mechanically, just as the child, when his body is completed and able to live apart, leaves its mother's womb. Sometimes the phantom becomes a rebellious son and one hears of uncanny struggles that have taken place between magicians and their creatures, the former being severely hurt or even killed by the latter.

Tibetan magicians also relate cases in which the Tulpa is sent to fulfill a mission, but does not come back and pursues its peregrinations as a half-conscious, dangerously mischievous puppet. The same thing, it is said, may happen when the maker of the Tulpa dies before having dissolved it. Yet, as a rule, the phantom either disappears suddenly at the death of the magician or gradually vanishes like a body that perishes for want of food.

Tulpas Storm the Internet

According to Nathan Thompson, whose September 3, 2014 article for *Vice* "Meet the 'Tulpamancers': The Internet's Newest Subculture Is Incredibly Weird," addressed the growing interest in Tulpas. "In 2009, the subject of Tulpas appeared on the discussion boards of 4chan. A few anonymous members started to experiment with creating Tulpas and fans of 'My Little Pony: Friendship is Magic' – known as 'bronies' created a new forum on Reddit and crafted Tulpas based on their favorite characters from the show.

"The Reddit forum has 6000-plus members," writes Dr. Samuel Veissière, Visiting Professor of Transcultural Psychiatry, Cognitive Science and Anthropology at McGill

How To Read The Human Aura And Create An Intelligent Life Form

University in Montreal. His study is the first academic literature about contemporary Tulpamancy. "The Russian social networking site Vkontakte also boasts 6000+ members... [Although] actual numbers are difficult to estimate."

"The My Little Pony fandom was one of the first online communities to really grab hold of the Tulpa phenomenon," says Ele Cambria, a Tulpamancer from Warrensburg, Missouri. "Bronies are very accepting of weirdness; they have that mindset of, 'Wow, that's not normal; that's cool.' The [My Little Pony] characters evoke a simple goodness...what fan wouldn't want one for a friend?"

It wasn't long before Tulpamancy also started to attract manga and fantasy fans. "My Tulpa is called Jasmine," says Ele. "She's a human but from an alternative reality where she can do magic. I created her a dozen years ago for a fantasy series I write and then made her into a Tulpa."

From reading these descriptions it would seem that Tulpas are simply made-up characters, somewhat along the lines of the imaginary friends that many kids play with during their younger years. However, in Eastern traditions, Tulpas are more than imaginary friends. Tulpas are believed to be conscious beings with their own thoughts and desires and they're not completely under their host's control. Practitioners report their Tulpas doing new and surprising things.

"Tulpas are understood as mental constructs that have achieved sentience," Dr. Veissière says. Nearly 40 percent of his respondents reported that their Tulpas "felt as real as a physical person", while 50.6 percent described them as "somewhat real... distinct from [their] own thoughts."

In Dion Fortune's book, ***Psychic Self-Defense,*** she mentions a wolf spirit that was tormenting her. This wolf it turned out was nothing more than a creation of her own will. It is also an incredible example of a Tulpa, with the exception that the wolf was never bound to her will.

A Tulpa can take on any idea, shape or purpose...the more complex the purpose, the more focus and energy required. A Tulpa created with a given purpose, such as protection; will be more effective than one whose purpose is to protect, warn, or even expedite services.

Some have asked if some thoughtforms have a reality of their own, separate of the human mind...such as an elemental. Theosophists and clairvoyants Annie Besant and C. W. Leadbeater placed thoughtforms in three classifications: (1) the image of the thinker; (2) an image of a material object associated with the thought; and (3) an independent image expressing the inherent qualities of the thought. Thoughts which are of a low nature, such as anger, hate, lust, greed, and so on, create thoughtforms which are dense in color and form. Thought of a more spiritual nature tend to generate forms possessing a greater purity, clarity, and refinement.

Thoughtforms then exist in either the mental or astral plane. Each entity is created from thought. Every thought is said to generate vibrations in the aura's mental body, which assume a floating form and colors depending on the nature and intensity of the thought. These thoughtforms are usually seen by clairvoyants; and may be not only intuitively sensed by others, but actually seen as physical entities.

Taking all of this into consideration, it is not unreasonable to consider that ALL spiritual entities, not considered to be human spirits may be constructs of the human mind...astral beings, elementals, angels, deities etc. Could this also explain other things such as cyrptid creatures along the lines of Bigfoot, lake monsters, or even UFOs? Could all of these things be creations of the worlds group mind?

Thoughtforms can occur spontaneously. "Group minds" that emerge whenever a group of people concentrate on the same thought, ideas, or goals, such as a team of employees or a crowd of demonstrators. To a certain extent the group-mind possesses the group; such is seen in psychic bonding and power that coalesces in crowds, and in the synergy of a close-knit working group. Usually when the group disbands the power of the group-mind dissipates too.

If enough people believe in gods such as Zeus, or Odin, then those beings can take on a life of their own. There are old stories, mistakenly categorized as mythologies, where people actually had personal encounters with their deities, much like people today say that under times of great personal difficulty that they saw and spoke with angels or even Jesus.

We are not here to say that one's religious beliefs are wrong. Instead, we are suggesting that our combined personal beliefs may have a hand in creating spiritual beings that take on the role of ghosts, demons and even gods. While the actual creative force in this and all other realities is far too complex for our minds to conceive. Thus, we create our gods that our in OUR own image, not the other way around.

The Creation of Philip

One famous attempt to create a Tulpa was conducted in 1973 by members of the Society of Psychical Research in Toronto. The objective of the group was to create a fictional character, which they named "Philip," and through a purposeful methodology, they attempted to contact the fictional entity and receive readily-apparent communications from it in return.

How To Read The Human Aura And Create An Intelligent Life Form

The group created a biography along with a sketch, to put a face on their fictional being. They then began formal weekly sittings in the "Philip room" where they sat together and discussed Philip and his life, meditated on his being, and attempted to create a "collective hallucination" of his spirit. During the early sessions, the group sought to create a common mental picture of Philip and his surroundings, focusing on his appearance and day-to-day activities.

The group's sessions continued for several months with no results until it was suggested that the lights be turned off to create an atmosphere that was less academic and more conducive to the summoning of ghostly spirits. Just as if they were having a traditional séance, group members sat around the table, placing their fingers lightly on the surface, and called for Philip to appear.

Shortly afterwards, a loud rap echoed through the room. Members of the team noted later that the rap was distinctive, clear, and so violent that the table itself vibrated. This was followed by a number of distinctive knocks. After these first communications from "Philip," the group began querying the entity, agreeing on a "one rap for yes, two for no."

After this point the group began to experience a wide range of paranormal events that has never been explained scientifically. Philip began producing extraordinary visible physical manifestations. In response to questions, group members began to hear whispers in their ears. In one of the early sessions, the group was stunned when the table suddenly, and violently, jumped and slid across the floor. At one point the table began to "dance," tilting onto a single leg and spinning about with the group members frantically running in a circle in an attempt to keep their fingers in place.

How To Read The Human Aura And Create An Intelligent Life Form

Philip even seemed to display emotions of his own. He refused to answer certain questions, saying they were too personal. It even seemed that his feelings could be hurt. In one session a group member told him that he could be sent away and replaced. Afterwards, Philip's activity began to tail off.

In conclusion the experimenters were never able to prove the "how" and the "why" behind Philip's manifestation. Did they conjure up an actual entity that simply latched onto the Philip story? Or, was Philip a direct result of the group's collective subconscious manifesting a thoughtform...a Tulpa?

We are permanently exchanging energies with our environment, the same way as we inhale and exhale air, ingest liquids and foodstuff. In our present framework of existence, no life is possible without exchange. This exchange of energies is what makes the creation of Tulpas possible.

The human aura is the manifestation of spiritual energies. Without the proper understanding of the human aura, the proper creation of a Tulpa will be an arduous journey, if not outright impossible.

How To Read The Human Aura And Create An Intelligent Life Form

The human aura is an energy field that surrounds, penetrates and extends out beyond the physical body, that is electromagnetic, electric and magnetic and is made up of varying types of live and intelligent vibrations or frequencies.

How To Read The Human Aura And Create An Intelligent Life Form

CHAPTER I
WHAT IS THE HUMAN AURA?

THE above question is frequently asked the student of occultism by someone who has heard the term but who is unfamiliar with its meaning. Simple as the question may seem, it is by no means easy to answer it, plainly and clearly in a few words, unless the hearer already has a general acquaintance with the subject of occult science. Let us commence at the beginning, and consider the question from the point of view of the person who has just heard the term for the first time.

The dictionaries define the word aura as: "Any subtle, invisible emanation or exhalation." The English authorities, as a rule, attribute the origin of the word to a Latin term meaning "air," but the Hindu authorities insist that it had its origin in the Sanscrit root _Ar_, meaning the spoke of a wheel, the significance being perceived when we remember the fact that the human aura radiates from the body of the individual in a manner similar to the radiation of the spokes of a wheel from the hub thereof. The Sanscrit origin of the term is the one preferred by occultists, although it will be seen that the idea of an aerial emanation, indicated by the Latin root, is not foreign to the real significance of the term.

Be the real origin of the term what it may, the idea of the human aura is one upon which all occultists are in full agreement and harmony, and the mention of which is found in all works upon the general subject of occultism. So we shall begin by a consideration of the main conception thereof, as held by all advanced occultists, ancient and modern, omitting little points of theoretical variance between the different schools.

Briefly, then, the human aura may be described as a fine, ethereal radiation or emanation surrounding each and every living human being. It extends from two to three feet, in all directions, from the body. It assumes an oval shape--a great egg-shaped nebula surrounding the body on all sides for a distance of two or three feet. This aura is sometimes referred to, in ordinary terms, as the "psychic atmosphere" of a person, or as his "magnetic atmosphere."

This atmosphere or aura is apparent to a large percentage of persons in the sense of the psychic awareness generally called "feeling," though the term is not a clear one. The majority of persons are more or less aware of that subtle something about the personality of others, which can be sensed or felt in a clear though unusual way when the other persons are nearby, even though they may be out of the range of the vision. Being outside of the ordinary range of the five senses, we are apt to feel that there is something queer or uncanny about these feelings of projected personality. But every person, deep in his heart, knows them to be realities and admits their effect upon his impressions regarding the persons from whom they emanate. Even small children, infants even, perceive this influence, and respond to it in the matter of likes and dislikes.

But, human testimony regarding the existence and character of the human aura does not stop with the reports of the psychic senses to which we have just referred. There are many individuals of the race--a far greater percentage than is generally imagined--who have the gift of psychic sight more or

How To Read The Human Aura And Create An Intelligent Life Form

less developed. Many persons have quite a well-developed power of this kind, who do not mention it to their acquaintances for fear of ridicule, or of being thought "queer." In addition to these persons, there are here and there to be found well-developed, clear-sighted, or truly clairvoyant persons, whose powers of psychic perception are as highly developed as are the ordinary senses of the average individual. And, the reports of these persons, far apart in time and space though they may be, have always agreed on the main points of psychic phenomena, particularly in regards to the human aura.

To the highly developed clairvoyant vision, every human being is seen as surrounded by the egg-shaped aura of two or three feet in depth, more dense and thick in the portion nearest the body, and then gradually becoming more tenuous, thin and indistinct as the distance from the body is increased. By the psychic perception, the aura is seen as a luminous cloud--a phosphorescent flame—deep and dense around the centre and then gradually shading into indistinctness toward the edges. As a matter of fact, as all developed occultists know, the aura really extends very much further than even the best clairvoyant vision can perceive it, and its psychic influence is perceptible at quite a distance in many cases. In this respect it is like any flame on the physical plane—it gradually fades into indistinctness, its rays persisting far beyond the reach of the vision, as may be proved by means of chemical apparatus, etc.

To the highly developed clairvoyant vision, the human aura is seen to be composed of all the colors of the spectrum, the combinations of colors differing in various persons, and constantly shifting in the case of every person. These colors reflect the mental (particularly the emotional) states of the person in whose aura they are manifested. Each mental state has its own particular combination formed from the few elementary colors which represent the elementary mental conditions. As the mind is ever shifting and changing its states, it follows that there will ever be a corresponding series of shifting changes in the colors of the human aura.

The shades and colors of the aura present an ever changing kaleidoscopic spectacle, of wonderful beauty and most interesting character. The trained occultist is able to read the character of any person, as well as the nature of his passing thoughts and feelings, by simply studying the shifting colors of his aura. To the developed occultist the mind and character become as an open book, to be studied carefully and intelligently.

Even the student of occultism, who has not been able to develop the clairvoyant vision to such a high degree, is soon able to develop the sense of psychic perception whereby he is able to at least "feel" the vibrations of the aura, though he may not see the colors, and thus be able to interpret the mental states which have caused them. The principle is of course the same, as the colors are but the outward appearance of the vibrations themselves, just as the ordinary colors on the physical plane are merely the outward manifestation of vibration of matter.

But it must not be supposed that the human aura is always perceived in the appearance of a luminous cloud of ever-changing color. When we say that such is its characteristic appearance, we mean it in the same sense that we describe the ocean as a calm, deep body of greenish waters. We know, however, that at times the ocean presents no such appearance, but, instead, is seen as rising in great mountainous waves, white capped, and threatening the tiny vessels of men with its power. Or again, we may define the word "flame" in the sense of a steady bright stream of burning gas, whereas, we know only too well, that the word also indicates the great hot tongues of fiery force that stream out from the windows of a burning building, and lick to destruction all with which it comes in contact.

So it is with the human aura. At times it may be seen as a beautiful, calm, luminous atmosphere, presenting the appearance of a great opal under the rays of the sun. Again, it blazes like the flames of a great furnace, shooting forth great tongues of fire in this direction and that, rising and falling in great waves of emotional excitement, or passion, or perhaps whirling like a great fiery maelstrom toward its centre, or swirling in an outward movement away from its centre. Again it may be seen as projecting from its depths smaller bodies or centres of mental vibration, which like sparks from a furnace detach themselves from the parent flame, and travel far away in other directions--these are the projected thought-forms of which all occultists are fond of speaking and which make plain many strange psychic occurrences.

So, it will be seen, the human aura is a very important and interesting phase of the personality of every individual. The psychic phase of man is as much the man himself as is the physical phase--the complete man being made up of the two phases. Man invisible is as much the real man as is man visible. As the finer forms of nature are always the most powerful, so is the psychic man more potent than the physical man.

In this book, I speak of the human aura, and its colors, as being perceived by astral or clairvoyant vision, for this is the way in which it is perceived and studied by the occultist. The occult teaching is that, in the evolution of the race, this astral vision will eventually become the common property of every human being--it so exists even now, and needs only development to perfect it.

How To Read The Human Aura And Create An Intelligent Life Form

But modern physical science is today offering corroborative proof (though the same is not needed by the occultist who has the astral vision) to the general public, of the existence of the human aura. In Europe, especially, a number of scientists have written on the subject of the aura, and have described the result of the experiments in which the aura has been perceived, and even photographed, by means of fluorescent screens, such as are used in taking X-Ray photographs, etc. Leading authorities in England, France, and still more recently, in Germany, have reported the discovery (!) of a nebulous, hazy, radio-active energy or substance, around the body of human beings. In short, they now claim that every human being is radio-active, and that the auric radiation may be registered and perceived by means of a screen composed of certain fluorescent material, interposed between the eye of the observer, and the person observed.

This aura, so discovered (!) by the scientists, is called by them the "human atmosphere," and is classified by them as similar to the radiations of other radio-active substances, radium, for instance. They have failed to discover color in this atmosphere, however, and know nothing, apparently, of the relation between auric colors and mental and emotional states, which are so familiar to every advanced occultist. I mention this fact merely as a matter of general interest and information to the student, and not as indicating, even in the slightest degree, any idea on my part that the old occult teaching, and the observed phenomena accompanying the same, regarding the human aura, require any proof or backing up on the part of material scientists. On the contrary, I feel that material science should feel flattered by the backing up by occult science of the new discovery (!) of the "human atmosphere." A little later on, material science may also discover (!) the auric colors, and announce the same to the wondering world, as a new truth.

How To Read The Human Aura And Create An Intelligent Life Form

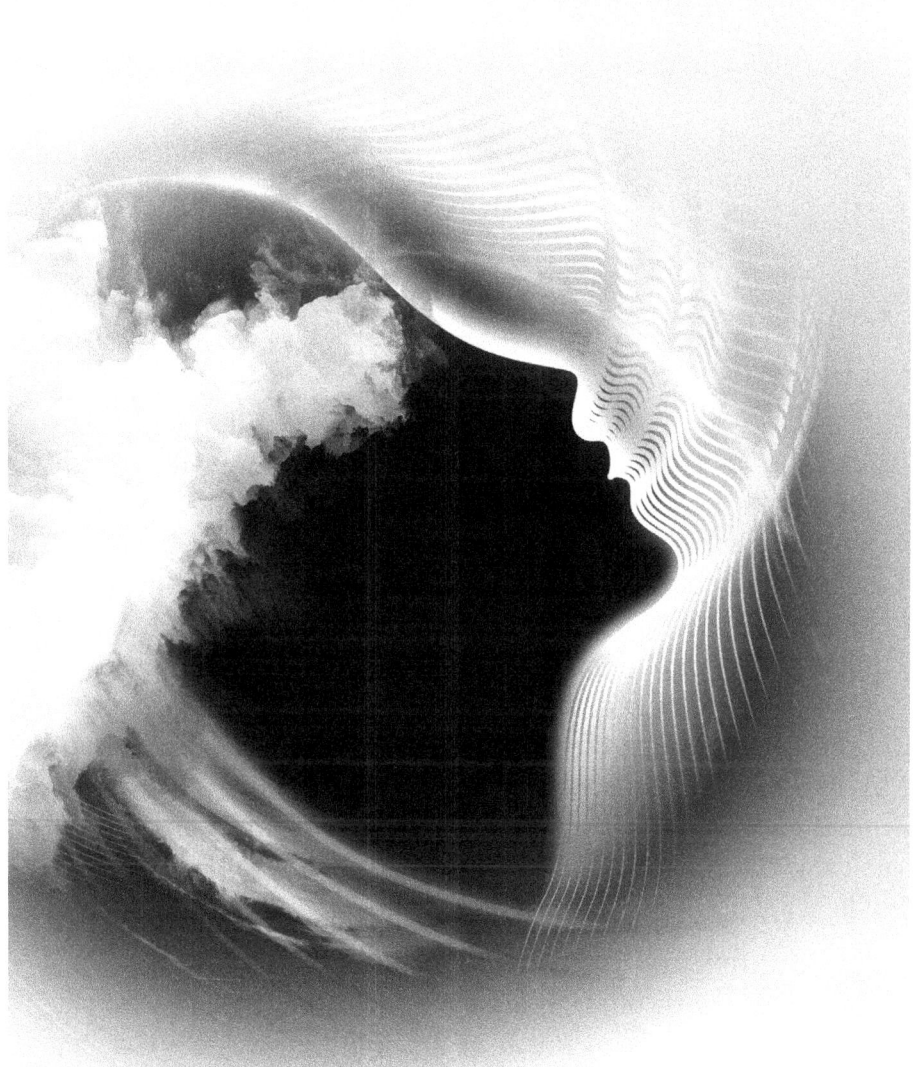

Auras contain all the primary colors of the rainbow at any given time and change color depending on the emotion an individual is experiencing. Our auras are made up of may colors and many shades of colors that are constantly changing. This reflects the constant change in our thoughts and emotions.

CHAPTER II

THE PRANA-AURA

MANY writers on the subject of the human aura content themselves with a description of the colors of the mental or emotional aura, and omit almost any reference whatsoever to the basic substance or power of the aura. This is like the play of Hamlet, with the character of Hamlet omitted, for, unless we understand something concerning the fundamental substance of which the aura is composed, we cannot expect to arrive at a clear understanding of the phenomena which arises from and by reason of the existence of this fundamental substance. We might as well expect a student to understand the principles of color, without having been made acquainted with the principles of light.

The fundamental substance of which the human aura is composed is none other than that wonderful principle of nature of which one reads so much in all occult writings, which has been called by many names, but which is perhaps best known under the Sanskrit term, _Prana_, but which may be thought of as Vital Essence, Life Power, etc.

It is not necessary in this book to go into the general consideration of the nature and character of Prana. It is sufficient for us to consider it in its manifestation of Vital Force, Life Essence, etc. In its broadest sense, Prana really is the Principle of Energy in Nature, but in its relation to living forms it is the Vital Force which lies at the very basis of manifested Life. It exists in all forms of living things, from the most minute microscopic form up to living creatures on higher planes, as much higher than man as man is higher than the simple microscopic life-forms. It permeates them all, and renders possible all life activity and functioning.

Prana is not the mind or the soul, but is rather the force or energy through which the soul manifests activity, and the mind manifests thought. It is the steam that runs the physical and mental machinery of life. It is the substance of the human aura, and the colors of mental states are manifested in that substance, just as the colors of chemical bodies are manifested in the substance of water. But Prana is not material substance-- it is higher than mere matter, being the underlying substance of Energy or Force in Nature.

While it is true, as we have seen, that all auras are composed of the substance of Prana, it is likewise true that there is a simple and elementary form of auric substance to which occultists have given the simple name of the prana-aura in order to distinguish it from the more complex forms and phases of the human aura. The simplicity of the character of the prana-aura causes it to be more readily sensed or perceived than is possible in the case of the more complex phases or forms of the aura. For whereas it is only the more sensitive organisms that can distinguish the finer vibrations of the mental and emotional aura, and only the clairvoyant sight which can discern its presence by its colors, almost any person, by a little careful experimenting, may become aware of the presence of the prana-aura, not only in the way of "feeling" it, but in many cases of actually seeing it with the ordinary vision rightly directed.

That which is known as the prana-aura is of course the most simple form or phase of the human aura. It is the form or phase which is more closely bound up with the physical body, and is less concerned with the mental states. This fact has caused some writers to speak of it as the "health aura," or "physical aura," both of which terms are fittingly applied as we shall see, although we prefer the simpler term we have used here, i. e., the prana-aura. For the prana-aura does show the state of the health of the individual radiating it, and it also really contains physical power and magnetism which may be, and is imparted to others.

The basic prana-aura is practically colorless, that is to say, it is about the color of the clearest water or a very clear diamond. By the clairvoyant vision it is seen to be streaked or marked by very minute, bristle-like lines, radiating outward from the physical body of the individual, in a manner very like "the quills upon the fretful porcupine," as Shakespeare puts it. In the case of excellent physical health, these bristle-like streaks are stiff and brittle-looking, whereas, if the general health of the person be deficient these bristle-like radiations seem to be more or less tangled, twisted, or curly; and, in some cases present a drooping appearance, and in extreme cases present the appearance of soft, limp fur.

It may interest the student to know that minute particles of this prana-aura, or vital magnetism, is sloughed off the body in connection with physical exhalations such as scent, etc., and remain in existence for some time after the person has passed from the particular place at which they were cast off. In fact, as all occultists know, it is these particles of the prana-aura which serve to give vitality to the "scent" of living creatures, which enables dogs and other animals to trace up the track of the person, or animal, for a long time after the person has passed. It is not alone the physical odor, which must be very slight as you will see upon a moment's consideration. It is really the presence of the particles of the prana-aura which enables the dog to distinguish the traces of one person among that of thousands of others, and the feat is as much psychical as physical.

Another peculiarity of the prana-aura is that it is filled with a multitude of extremely minute sparkling particles, resembling tiny electric sparks, which are in constant motion. These sparks, which are visible to persons of only slightly developed psychic power, impart a vibratory motion to the prana-aura which, under certain conditions is plainly visible to the average person. This vibratory movement is akin to the movement of heated air arising from a hot stove, or from the heated earth on a mid-summer day.

If the student will close his eyes partially, until he peers out from narrowed lids, and then will closely observe some very healthy person sitting in a dim light, he may perceive this undulating, pulsing vibration extending an inch or two from the surface of the body. It requires some little knack to recognize these vibrations, but a little practice will often give one the key; and after the first recognition, the matter becomes easy.

Again, in the case of persons of active brains, one may perceive this pulsating prana-aura around the head of the person, particularly when he is engaged in concentrated active thought. A little practice will enable almost anyone to perceive faintly the dim outlines of the prana-aura around his own fingers and hand, by placing his hand against a black background, in a dim light, and then gazing at it with narrowed eye-lids, squinting if necessary. Under these circumstances, after a little practice, one will be apt to perceive a tiny outlined aura, or radiation, or halo, of pale yellowish light surrounding the hand.

By extending the fingers, fan shape, you will perceive that each finger is showing its own little outlined prana-aura. The stronger the vital force, the plainer will be the perception of the phenomenon. Often the prana-aura, in these experiments, will appear like the semi-luminous radiance surrounding a candle flame or gas light. Under the best conditions, the radiation will assume an almost phosphorescent appearance. Remember, this is simply a matter of trained ordinary sight,--not clairvoyant vision.

This prana-aura is identical with human magnetism, which is employed in ordinary magnetic healing. That is to say it is the outer manifestation of the wonderful pranic force. It is felt when you shake hands, or otherwise come in close physical contact with a strongly magnetic person. On the other hand it is what the weakly, human vampire-like persons unconsciously, or consciously, try to draw off from strong persons, if the latter allow them so to do from want of knowledge of self protection. Who has not met persons of this kind, who seem to sap one's very life force away from him? Remember, then, that the prana-aura is the aura or radiation of life force, or vital power, which is the steam of your living activity, physical and mental. It is the pouring out of the vital "steam" which is running your vital machinery. Its presence indicates Life--its absence Lifelessness.

CHAPTER III

THE ASTRAL COLORS

THE term "astral," so frequently employed by all occultists, is difficult to explain or define except to those who have pursued a regular course of study in occult science. For the purpose of the present consideration, it is enough to say that over and above the ordinary physical sense plane there is another and more subtle plane, known as the Astral Plane. Every human being possesses the innate and inherent faculty of sensing the things of this astral plane, by means of an extension or enlargement of the powers of the ordinary senses, so to speak. But, in the majority of persons in the present stage of development, these astral senses are lying dormant, and only here and there do we find individuals who are able to sense on the astral plane, although in the course of evolution the entire race will be able to do so, of course. The colors of the human aura, mentioned in the preceding two chapters, and which arise from the various mental and emotional states, belong to the phenomena of the astral plane, and hence bear the name of "the astral colors." Belonging to the astral plane, and not to the ordinary physical plane, they are perceived only by the senses functioning on the astral plane, and are invisible to the ordinary physical plane sight. But, to those who have developed the astral sight, or clairvoyance, these colors are as real as are the ordinary colors to the average person, and their phenomena have been as carefully recorded by occult science as have the physical plane colors by physical science. The fact that to the ordinary physical senses they are invisible, does not render them any the less real. Remember, in this connection, that to the blind man our physical colors do not exist. And, for that matter, the ordinary colors do not exist to "color blind" persons. The ordinary physical plane person is simply "color blind" to the astral colors--that's all.

On the astral plane each shade of mental or emotional state has its corresponding astral color, the latter manifesting when the form appears. It follows then, of course, that when once the occultist has the key to this color correspondence, and thus is able to perceive the astral colors by means of his astral vision, he also is able to read the mental and emotional states of any person within the range of his vision, as easily as you are now reading the printed words of this book.

Before proceeding to a consideration of the list of astral colors in the human aura, I wish to call your attention to a slight variation in the case of the prana-aura, of which I have spoken in our last chapter. I have stated therein that the prana-aura is colorless like a diamond or clear water. This is true in the average case, but in the case of a person of very strong physical vitality or virility, the prana-aura takes on, at times, a faint warm pink tinge, which is really a reflection from the red astral color, of the meaning of which color you shall now learn.

Like their physical plane counterparts, all the astral colors are formed from three Primary Colors, namely (1) Red; (2) Blue; and (3) Yellow. From these three primary colors, all other colors are formed. Following the Primary Colors, we find what are known as the Secondary Colors, namely: (1) Green, derived from a combination of Yellow and Blue; (2) Orange, formed from a combination of Yellow and Red; and (3) Purple, formed from a combination of Red and Blue. Further combinations produce the other colors, as for instance, Green and Purple form Olive; Orange and Purple form Russet; Green and Orange form Citrine.

Black is called an absence of color, while White is really a harmonious blending of all colors, strange as this may appear to one who has not studied the subject. The blending of the Primary Colors in varied proportions produce what is known as the "hues" of color. Adding white to the hues, we obtain "tints;" while mixing Black produces "shades." Strictly speaking Black and White are known as "neutral" colors.

Now for the meaning of the astral colors--that is, the explanation of the mental or emotional state represented by each. I ask that the student familiarize himself with the meaning of the Primary Colors and their combinations. A clear understanding of the key of the astral colors is often an aid in the development of astral sight.

KEY TO THE ASTRAL COLORS

RED. Red represents the physical phase of mentality. That is to say, it stands for that part of the mental activities which are concerned with physical life. It is manifested by the vitality of the body, and in other hues, tints and shades, is manifested by passions, anger, physical cravings, etc. I shall describe the various forms of Red manifestation, a little later on.

BLUE. Blue represents the religious, or spiritual, phase of mentality. That is to say, it stands for that part of the mental activities which are concerned with high ideals, altruism, devotion, reverence, veneration, etc. It is manifested, in its various hues, tints, and shades, by all forms of religious feeling and emotion, high and low, as we shall see as we proceed.

YELLOW. Yellow represents the intellectual phase of mentality. That is to say, it stands for that part of the mental activities which are concerned with reasoning, analysis, judgment, logical processes, induction, deduction, synthesis, etc. In its various hues, tints and shades, it is manifested by the various forms of intellectual activity, high and low, as we shall see as we proceed.

WHITE. White stands for what occultists know as Pure Spirit, which is a very different thing from the religious emotion of "spirituality," and which really is the essence of the ALL that really is. Pure Spirit is the positive pole of Being. We shall see the part played by it in the astral colors, as we proceed.

BLACK. Black stands for the negative pole of Being--the very negation of Pure Spirit, and opposing it in every way. We shall see the part played by it in the astral colors as we proceed.

The various combinations of the three Astral Primary Colors are formed in connection with Black and White as well as by the blending of the three themselves. These combinations, of course, result from the shades of mental and emotional activity manifested by the individuality, of which they are the reflection and the key.

The combinations and blending of the astral colors, however, are numberless, and present an almost infinite variety. Not only is the blending caused by the mixing of the colors themselves, in connection with black and white, but in many cases the body of one color is found to be streaked, striped, dotted or clouded by other colors. At times there is perceived the mixture of two antagonistic color streams fighting against each other before blending. Again we see the effect of one color neutralizing another.

In some cases great black clouds obscure the bright colors beneath, and then darken the fierce glow of color, just as is often witnessed in the case of a physical conflagration. Again, we find great flashes of bright yellow, or red, flaring across the field of the aura, showing agitation or the conflict of intellect and passion.

The average student, who has not developed the astral vision, is inclined to imagine that the astral colors in the human aura present the appearance of an egg-shaped rainbow, or spectrum, or something of that sort. But this is a great mistake. In the first place, the astral colors are seldom at rest, for all mental and emotional activity is the result of vibration, change, and rhythmic motion. Consequently, the colors of the aura present a kaleidoscopic appearance, of constant change of color, shape and grouping--a great electrical display, so to speak, constantly shifting, changing, and blending.

Great tongues of flame-like emanations project themselves beyond the border of the aura, under strong feeling or excitement, and great vibratory whirls and swirls are manifested. The sight is most fascinating, although somewhat terrifying at first. Nature is wise in bestowing the gift of astral vision slowly and almost imperceptibly.

CHAPTER IV
THE ASTRAL COLORS (Continued)

REMEMBERING, always, the significance of the three primary colors on the astral plane, let us consider the meaning of the combinations, shades, hues, and tints of these colors.

THE RED GROUP. In this group of astral colors seen in the human aura, we find strongly in evidence the clear bright red shade, similar to that of fresh, pure arterial blood as it leaves the heart, filled with pure material freshly oxygenated. This shade, in the aura, indicates health, life-force, vigor, virility, etc., in pure and untainted form. The aura of a healthy, strong child shows this shade of color very plainly and strongly.

Strong, pure natural emotions, such as friendship, love of companionship, love of physical exercise, healthy clean sports, etc., are manifested by a clear clean shade of red. When these feelings become tainted with selfishness, low motives, etc., the shade grows darker and duller.

Love of low companionship, unclean sports, or selfish games, etc., produce an unpleasant muddy red shade. A shade of red, very near to crimson, is the astral color of Love, but the tint and shade varies greatly according to the nature of this form of emotional feeling. A very high form of love, which seeks the good of the loved one, rather than the satisfaction of oneself, manifests as a beautiful rose tint—one of the most pleasing of the astral tints, by the way. Descending in the scale, we find the crimson shade becoming darker and duller, until we descend to the plane of impure, sensual, coarse passion, which is manifested by an ugly, dull, muddy crimson of a repulsive appearance, suggesting blood mixed with dirty earth or barnyard soil.

A peculiar series of red shades are those manifesting anger in its various forms, from the vivid scarlet flashes of anger color, arising from what may be called "righteous indignation," down the scale to the ugly flashes of deep, dull red, betokening rage and uncontrolled passion. The red of anger generally shows itself in flashes, or great leaping flames, often accompanied by a black background, in the case of malicious hate, or by a dirty, greenish background when the rage arises from jealousy, or envy. The color of avarice is a very ugly combination of dull, dark red, and a dirty ugly green. If persons could see their own astral colors accompanying these undesirable mental states, the sight would perhaps so disgust them with such states as to work a cure. At any rate, they are most disgusting and repulsive to the occultist who beholds them in the human aura, and he often wonders why they do not sicken the person manifesting them--they often do just this thing, to tell the truth.

THE YELLOW GROUP. In this group of astral colors seen in the human aura we find as many varieties as we do in the red group. Yellow, denoting intellect, has many degrees of shade and tint, and many degrees of clearness.

An interesting shade in this group is that of Orange, which represents different forms of "pride of intellect," intellectual ambition, love of mastery by will, etc. The greater degree of red in the astral orange color, the greater the connection with the physical or animal nature. Pride and love of power over others, has much red in its astral color, while love of intellectual mastery has much less red in its composition.

Pure intellectual attainment, and the love of the same, is manifested by a beautiful clear golden yellow. Great teachers often have this so strongly in evidence, that at times their students have glimpses of a golden "halo" around the head of the teacher. Teachers of great spirituality have this "nimbus" of golden yellow, with a border of beautiful blue tint, strongly in evidence.

The paintings of the great spiritual teachers of the race usually have this radiance pictured as a "halo," showing a recognition of the phenomenon on the part of the great artists. Hoffman's celebrated painting of the Christ in the Garden of Gethsemane shows this nimbus so accurately depicted that the occultist is convinced that this artist must have actually witnessed a similar scene in the astral light, so true to the astral facts are its details. The images of the Buddha also show this radiance.

The rich golden shades of intellectual yellow are comparatively rare, a sickly lemon color being the only indication of intellectual power and found in the aura of the great run of persons. To the sight of the occultist, employing his power of astral vision, a crowd of persons will manifest here and there, at widely separated points, the bright golden yellow of the true intellect, appearing like scattered lighted candles among a multitude of faintly burning matches.

THE GREEN GROUP. This is a peculiar group, consisting as of course it does of various combinations of blues and yellows, tinted and shaded by white or black. Even skilled occultists find it very difficult to account for the fact of certain green shades arising from the spiritual blue and the intellectual yellow—this is one of the most obscure points in the whole subject of the astral colors, and none but the most advanced occultists are able to explain the "why" in some instances. To those who are fond of analysis of this kind, I will drop the following hint, which may help them out in the matter, viz. The key is found in the fact that Green lies in the centre of the astral spectrum, and is a balance between the two extremes, and is also influenced by these two extremes in a startling manner.

A certain restful green denotes love of nature, out of door life, travel in the country, etc., and also, slightly differing in tint, the love of home scenes, etc. Again, a clear beautiful lighter tint of green indicates what may be called sympathy, altruistic emotion, charity, etc. Again, illustrating variety in this group of astral colors, another shade of green shows intellectual tolerance of the views of others. Growing duller, this indicates tact, diplomacy, ability to handle human nature, and descending another degree or so blends into insincerity, shiftiness, untruth, etc. There is an ugly slate-colored green indicating low, tricky deceit—this is a very common shade in the colors of the average aura, I am sorry to say. Finally, a particularly ugly, muddy, murky green indicates jealousy and kindred feelings, envious malice, etc.

THE BLUE GROUP. This interesting group of astral colors represents the varying forms and degrees of religious emotion, "spirituality," etc. The highest form of spiritual, religious feeling and thought is represented by a beautiful, rich, clear violet tint, while the lower and more gross phases of religious emotion and thought are represented by the darker and duller hues, tints, and shades until a deep, dark indigo is reached, so dark that it can scarcely be distinguished from a bluish black. This latter color, as might be expected, indicates a low superstitious form of religion, scarcely worthy of the latter name. Religion, we must remember, has its low places as well as its heights—its garden grows the rarest flowers, and at the same time the vilest weeds.

High spiritual feelings—true spiritual unfoldment—is indicated by a wonderfully clear light blue, of an unusual tint, something akin to the clear light blue of the sky on a cool autumn afternoon, just before sunset. Even when we witness an approach to this color in Nature, we are inspired by an uplifting feeling as if we were in the presence of higher things, so true is the intuition regarding these things.

Morality, of a high degree, is indicated by a series of beautiful shades of blue, always of a clear inspiring tint. Religious feeling ruled by fear, is indicated by a shade of bluish gray. Purple denotes a love of form and ceremony, particularly those connected with religious offices or regal grandeur of a solemn kind. Purple, naturally, was chosen as the royal color in the olden days.

THE BROWN GROUP. The brown group of astral colors represents desire for gain and accumulation, ranging from the clear brown of industrious accumulation, to the murky dull browns of miserliness, greed and avarice. There is a great range in this group of brown shades, as may be imagined.

THE GRAY GROUP. The group of grays represents a negative group of thought and emotions. Gray represents fear, depression, lack of courage, negativity, etc. This is an undesirable and unpleasant group.

BLACK. Black, in the astral colors, stands for hatred, malice, revenge, and "devilishness" generally. It shades the brighter colors into their lower aspects, and robs them of their beauty. It stands for hate--also for gloom, depression, pessimism, etc.

WHITE. White is the astral color of Pure Spirit, as we have seen, and its presence raises the degree of the other colors, and renders them clearer. In fact, the perception of the highest degree of Being known to the most advanced occultist is manifested to the highest adepts and masters in the form of "The Great White Light," which transcends any light ever witnessed by the sight of man on either physical or astral plane--for it belongs to a plane higher than either, and is absolute, rather than a relative, white. The presence of white among the astral colors of the human aura, betokens a high degree of spiritual attainment and unfoldment, and when seen permeating the entire aura it is one of the Signs of the Master—the token of Adeptship.

CHAPTER V
THE AURIC KALEIDOSCOPE

AS we have seen, the human aura is never in a state of absolute rest or quiet. Motion and change is ever manifested by it. It has its periods of comparative calm, of course, but even in this state there is a pulsing, wave-like motion apparent. The clouds of changing color fly over its surface, and in its depth, like the fast driven fleecy clouds over the summer sky, illumined by the rays of the setting sun.

Again, fierce storms of mental activity, or emotional stress, disturb its comparative calm, and the wildest scenes are witnessed in the aura by the observer. So intense are the vibrations of some of these mental storms that their effect is plainly felt by the average person, though he is not able to distinguish the colors or the great whirls and swirls of auric substance accompanying them.

A person sunk in reverie, dream-states, or sleep, presents an interesting auric kaleidoscope, which possesses great beauty if the person be normal and of average morality. In such a case there is a cloudy-clearness (if the term may be used) tinged with tints and shades of varying colors, blending in strange and interesting combinations, appearing gradually from previous combinations, and sinking gradually into new ones.

To the observer of the aura the term "opalescent" instinctively presents itself, for there is a striking resemblance to the opaline peculiar play of colors of delicate tints and shades in a body of pearly or milky hue. Color shades into color, tint into tint, hue into hue, as in the color scale of the spectrum of which the rainbow is the most familiar example. But the rainbow or spectrum lacks the peculiar semi-transparency of the auric colors, and also the constantly changing and dissolving body of colors of the aura.

At this point, I wish to call your attention to a phase of the aura which I purposely passed over in the preceding chapters. I allude to the phase of the aura which presents the "pearly" appearance of the opalescent body, which we have just noted. This appearance is manifested neither by any of the mental or emotional states, nor is it the prana-aura or vital force which I have described in a previous chapter. It is the manifestation of what is known to occultists as "etheric substance," and is a very interesting feature of the auric phenomena.

This etheric substance, which manifests this peculiar radiance in the body of the aura, composes that which is called by some occultists "the astral body," but this latter term is also employed in another sense, and I prefer to use the term "etheric double" to indicate what some others know as "the astral body." Etheric substance is much finer form of substance than that which composes the physical body. It is really matter in a very high degree of vibration--much higher than even the ultra-gaseous matter of physical substance. It may be sensed, ordinarily, only on the astral plane, which is its own particular plane of activity.

How To Read The Human Aura And Create An Intelligent Life Form

The etheric double, composed of this etheric substance, is the exact counterpart of its physical counterpart--the ordinary physical body of the individual--although it is capable of great expansion or shrinking in space. Like the physical body it radiates an aura, and this combining with the other forms of the auric body, gives to it its peculiar pearly appearance, which is the background of its opalescence previously noted.

The etheric double explains the phenomenon of spectral appearances or ghosts, for it persists for a time after the death of the physical body, and under some conditions becomes visible to the ordinary sight. It sometimes is projected from the physical body, and at such times appears as an apparition of the living, of which there are many cases recorded by the societies investigating psychical subjects.

The etheric double, or astral body, is referred to here, however, merely to explain the peculiar pearly tint of the background, or body, of the aura, in and through which the mental and emotional auric colors play and move. It may interest you, however, to know that this phase of aura is always present around and about a "ghost" or dematerialized disembodied soul, or "spirit" as common usage terms it.

The aura of the wide-awake person is, of course, far more active and more deeply colored than is that of the person in reverie, dream, or sleep. And, again the aura of the person manifesting a high degree of mental activity, or strong feeling or passion, is still brighter and deeper than the ordinary person performing his daily routine work. In the state of anger, or love-passion, for instance, the aura is violently disturbed, deep shades of color whirling and swirling in the depths and surface of the auric body. Lightning-like flashes shoot forth and great bodies of lurid smoky clouds fly on the surface. Looking into the aura of a man wild with rage and passion, is like peering into

Inferno. The astral plane, in the region of a lynching mob, or other body of persons filled with rage, becomes a frightful scene of auric radiation.

A person filled with the emotion of pure love, fills his aura with the most beautiful tints and shades of high rosy color, and to behold the same is a pleasure fully appreciated by the occultist. A church filled with persons of a high devotional ideality, is also a beautiful place, by reason of the mingling of auric violet-blue vibrations of those therein assembled. The atmosphere of a prison is most depressing and presents a most unpleasant appearance to one possessing the astral vision. Likewise the astral atmosphere of an abode of vice and passion, becomes really physically nauseating to the occultist of high ideals and taste. Such scenes on the astral plane are avoided by all true occultists, except when the call of duty leads them to visit them to give aid and help.

There are two distinct features connected with the auric coloring of every person. The first is the coloring resulting from the more habitual thoughts and feelings of the person--from his character, in fact; while the second is the coloring resulting from the particular feelings, or thoughts, manifested by him at that particular moment or time.

The color of the feeling of the moment soon disappears and fades away, while the more habitual feeling, bound up with his character, causes its corresponding color to abide more permanently, and thus to give a decided hue to his general auric color appearance.

The trained occultist is, therefore, able to ascertain not only the passing thoughts and feelings of a person, but also to determine infallibly his general character, tendencies, past character and actions, and general nature, simply from a careful examination and study of the auric colors of the person in question.

As all occultists well know, every place, dwelling, business place, church, courtroom--every village, city, country, nation--has its own collective aura, known as "astral atmosphere," which is simply but a combined reflection of the individual auras of the human units of which its body of inhabitants is made up. These atmospheric vibrations are plainly felt by many persons, and we are instinctively attracted or repelled by reason thereof. But, to the developed occultists, these places manifest the auric colors, in the combinations arising from the nature of the mentalities of the persons dwelling in them.

Each place has its collective aura, just as each person has his individual aura. The astral plane presents a wonderful scene of color by reason of this and similar causes. The harmony of the color scheme, in some cases, is marvelously beautiful; while the horrible aspect of scenes resemble a nightmare vision of the worst kind.

It is easy to understand why some of the ancients who stumbled into glimpses of the astral plane, while in dream-state or trance, reported the vision of terrible hells of unquenchable fire, fiery lakes of smoking brimstone, etc., for such ideas would naturally come to the mind of the uninformed person who had peered into the astral plane in such cases.

And, in the same way, the visions of heaven reported by the saints, and others of high spirituality, are explainable on the theory that these persons had sensed some of the beautiful scenes of the higher astral planes, filled with the combined auric tints and hues of souls of high development. The principle of auric colors holds good on all the many planes of being and existence--high as well as low.

How To Read The Human Aura And Create An Intelligent Life Form

I merely hint at a great occult truth in making the above statements. The thoughtful will be able to read between my lines. I have given you a little key which will unlock the door of many mysteries, if you will but use it intelligently.

CHAPTER VI

THOUGHT FORMS

THAT interesting phase of occult phenomena, known as "thought forms," is so closely related to the general subject of the human aura that a mention of one must naturally lead to the thought of the other. Thought-forms are built up of the very material composing the aura, and manifest all of the general characteristics thereof, even to the auric colors. An understanding of the facts of the human aura is necessary for a correct understanding of the nature of the thought-forms composed of the same substance.

A "thought form," or "Tulpa," is a peculiar manifestation of mental activity on the astral plane. It is more than a powerful disturbance in the body of the human aura, although this is the place of its embodiment or birth in the objective world. It is formed in the following manner: A person manifests a strong desire, feeling or idea, which is naturally filled with the dynamic force of his will. This sets up a series of strong vibrations in the body of the aura, which gradually resolve themselves into a strong whirling centre of thought-force involved in a mass of strongly cohesive auric substance, and strongly charged with the power of the prana of the person.

In some cases these thought forms survive in the auric body for some little time, and then gradually fade away. In other cases they survive and maintain an almost independent existence for some time, and exert a strong influence upon other persons coming in the presence of the person. Again, these thought forms may be so strongly charged with prana, and so imbued with the mental force of the person, that they will actually be thrown off and away from the aura itself, and travel in space until they exhaust their initial energy—in the meantime exerting an influence upon the psychic aura of other persons.

A thought form is more than merely a strongly manifested thought – it really is such a thought, but surrounded by a body of ethereal substance, charged with prana, and even carrying with it the vibration of the life energy of its creator. It is a child of the mind of its creator, and acquires a portion of his life-essence, so to speak, which abides with it for a longer or shorter time after its birth. In extreme instances it becomes practically a semi-living elemental force, of necessarily comparatively short life.

To those who find it difficult to understand how a thought form can persist after separation from the presence of the thinker, I would say that the phenomena is similar to that of light traveling in space, long after the star which originated it has been destroyed. Or, again, it is like the vibrations of heat remaining in a room after the lamp or stove causing it has been removed, or the fire in the grate having died out. Or like the sound waves of the drum-beat persisting after the beat itself has ceased. It is all a matter of the persistence of vibrations.

How To Read The Human Aura And Create An Intelligent Life Form

Thought forms differ greatly one from the other in the matter of shape and general appearance. The most common and simple form is that of an undulating wave, or series of tiny waves, resembling the circles caused by the dropping of a pebble into a still pond. Another form is that of a tiny rotating bit of cloud-like substance, sometimes whirling towards a central point, like a whirlpool; and sometimes swirling away from the central point like the familiar "pin-wheel" fireworks toy. Another form is akin the ring of smoke projected from the coughing locomotive, or the rounded lips of the cigar smoker, the movement in this kind being a form of spiral rotation. Other thought forms have the appearance of swiftly rotating balls of cloudy substance, often glowing with faint phosphorescence.

Sometimes the thought form will appear as a great slender jet, like steam ejected from the spout of a tea-kettle, which is sometimes broken up into a series of short, puffed-out jets, each following the jet preceding it, and traveling in a straight line. Sometimes the thought form shoots forth like a streak of dim light, almost resembling a beam of light flashed from a mirror. Occasionally, it will twist its way along like a long, slender corkscrew, or auger, boring into space.

In cases of thought-forms sent forth by explosive emotion, the thought form will actually take the form of a bomb, which literally explodes when it reaches the presence of the person toward whom it is aimed. Every person has experienced this feeling of a thought bomb having been exploded in his near vicinity, having been directed by a vigorous personality. This form is frequently found in the thought forms sent out by a strong, earnest, vigorous orator.

There are strong thought forms which seem to strive to push back the other person, so correctly do they represent the idea and feeling back of their manifestation. Others seem to strive to wind around the other person, and to try to literally drag him toward the first person, this form often accompanying strong appeal, persuasion, coaxing, etc., when accompanied by strong desire. A particularly vigorous form of this kind of thought form takes on the appearance of a nebulous octopus, with long, winding, clinging tentacles, striving to wrap around the other person, and to draw him toward the center.

The force of the feeling behind the manifestation of the thought form will often travel a long distance from the sender-- in fact, in cases of great power of concentration, space seems to be no barrier to its passage. In striking instances of thought transference, etc., it will be found that thought forms play an important part.

The variety of shapes of thought forms is almost endless. Each combination of thought and feeling creates its own form, and each individual seems to have his own peculiarities in this respect. The forms I have above described, however, will serve as typical cases to illustrate the more common classes of appearances. The list, however, might be indefinitely expanded from the experience of any experienced occultist, and is not intended to be full by any means. All varieties of geometrical forms are found among the thought forms, some of them being of remarkable beauty.

In considering the subject of projected thought forms, moreover, it must be remembered that they partake of, and manifest, the same colors as does the aura itself, for they are composed of the same material and are charged with the same energy. But, note this difference, that whereas the aura is energized from the constant battery of the organism of the individual, the thought form, on the contrary, has at its service only the energy with which it was charged when it was thrown off--being a storage battery, as it were, which in time expends all of its power and then is powerless.

Every thought form bears the same color that it would possess if it had been retained in the body of the aura itself. But, as a rule, the colors are plainer, and less blended with others--this because each thought form is the representation of a single definite feeling or thought, or group of same, instead of being a body of widely differing mental vibrations. Thus the thought form of anger will show its black and red, with its characteristic flashes. The thought form of passion will show forth its appropriate auric colors and general characteristics. The thought form of high ideal love will show its beautiful form and harmonious tinting, like a wonderful celestial flower from the garden of some far off Paradise.

Many thought forms never leave the outer limits of the aura, while others are projected to great distances. Some sputter out as they travel, and are disintegrated, while others continue to glow like a piece of heated iron, for many hours. Others persist for a long time, with a faint phosphorescent glow. A careful study of what has been said regarding the characteristics of the various feelings and emotions, as manifested in the auric body, will give the student a very fair general idea of what may be the appearance of any particular variety of thought form, for a general principle runs through the entire series of auric phenomena. An understanding of the fundamental principles will lead to an understanding of any of the particular varieties of the manifestation thereof.

Finally, remember this: A thought form is practically a bit of the detached aura of a person, charged with a degree of his prana, and energized with a degree of his life energy. So, in a limited sense, it really is a projected portion of his personality.

How To Read The Human Aura And Create An Intelligent Life Form

Tibetan Lore And Thought Form Creation

The stage from producing thought forms as internal hallucinations to an actual physical reality requires patience and a good understanding on the ability of the human mind to influence the subtle vibrations that make up the universe.

Alexandra David-Neel, in her 1931 book *"**With Mystics and Magicians in Tibet**,"* discussed how it was her intention to group together a certain number of salient points concerning the occult and mystical theories and the psychic training practices of the Tibetans. One of her most controversial subjects mentioned was the creation of intelligent thought forms, Tulpas.

The belief in the passing of some subtle self from one body to another, and even in its roaming about disembodied, was current in India. Such belief was not infrequent in Tibet, where the "translation" of the self from one body to another one is called trong jug (spelt: grong hjug.)

Possibly the theories regarding trong jug have been imported from India. Milarespa, in his autobiography, relates that his guru Marpa was not taught the secret of trong jug by his own teacher Narota, but when already old, made a journey to India to learn it.

It is to be noted that believers in the "translation" of an ethereal self or "double," generally depict the body from which it withdraws, as remaining inanimate. Here lies the essential difference between that supposed phenomenon and the apparitions, voluntary or unconsciously created, of a Tulpa, (Tulpa, spelt sprulpa, "magic, illusory creations.") either alike or different from its creator.

In fact, while the translation as related in Indian or Tibetan stories, may well be regarded as a fable, the creation of

How To Read The Human Aura And Create An Intelligent Life Form

Tulpas seems worthy of investigation. Phantoms, as Tibetans describe them, and those that I have myself seen do not resemble the apparitions which are said to occur during spiritualist séances.

In Tibet, the witnesses of these phenomena have not been especially invited to endeavor to produce them, or to meet a medium known for producing them. Consequently, their minds are not prepared and intent on seeing apparitions. There is no table upon which the company lay their hands nor any medium in trance, nor a dark closet in which the latter is shut up. Darkness is not required, sun and open air do not keep away the phantoms.

As I have said, some apparitions are created on purpose either by a lengthy process resembling that described in the former chapter on the visualization of Yidam or, in the case of proficient adepts, instantaneously or almost instantaneously.

In other cases, apparently the author of the phenomenon generates it unconsciously, and is not even in the least aware of the apparition being seen by others.

In connection with this kind of visualization or thought-form creation, I may relate a few phenomena which I have witnessed myself.

A young Tibetan who was in my service went to see his family. I had granted him three weeks' leave, after which he was to purchase a food supply, engage porters to carry the loads across the hills, and come back with the caravan. Most likely the fellow had a good time with his people. Two months elapsed and still he did not return. I thought he had definitely left me.

Then I saw him one night in a dream. He arrived at my place clad in a somewhat unusual fashion, wearing a sun hat of foreign shape. He had never worn such a hat. The next morning, one of my servants came to me in haste. "Wangdu has come back," he told me. "I have just seen him down the hill."

The coincidence was strange. I went out of my room to look at the traveler. The place where I stood dominated a valley. I distinctly saw Wangdu. He was dressed exactly as I had seen him in my dream. He was alone and walking slowly up the path that wound up the hill slope.

I remarked that he had no luggage with him and the servant who was next me answered: "Wangdu has walked ahead, the load-carriers must be following."

We both continued to observe the man. He reached a small chörten, walked behind it and did not reappear. The base of this chörten was a cube built in stone, less than three feet high, and from its needle-shaped top to the ground, the small monument was no more than seven feet high. There was no cavity in it.

Moreover, the chörten was completely isolated: there were neither houses, nor trees, nor undulations, nor anything that could provide a hiding in the vicinity.

My servant and I believed that Wangdu was resting for a while under the shade of the chörten. But as time went by without his reappearing, I inspected the ground round the monument with my field-glasses, but discovered nobody.

Very much puzzled I sent two of my servants to search for the boy. I followed their movements with the glasses but no trace was to be found of Wangdu nor of anybody else.

That same day a little before dusk the young man appeared in the valley with his caravan. He wore the very same dress and the foreign sun hat which I had seen in my dream, and in the morning vision.

How To Read The Human Aura And Create An Intelligent Life Form

Without giving him or the load-carriers time to speak with my servants and hear about the phenomenon, I immediately questioned them. From their answers I learned that all of them had spent the previous night in a place too far distant from my dwelling for anyone to reach the latter in the morning. It was also clearly stated that Wangdu had continually walked with the party.

During the following weeks I was able to verify the accuracy of the men's declarations by inquiring about the time of the caravan's departure, at the few last stages where the porters were changed. It was proved that they had all spoken the truth and had left the last stage together with Wangdu, as they said.

The other strange occurrence I have to relate belongs to the category of phenomena which are voluntarily produced. The fact that the apparition appeared in the likeness of the lama who caused it, must not lead us to think that he projected a subtle double of himself. This is not the opinion of advanced adepts in Tibetan secret lore.

According to them such phantoms are Tulpas, magic formations generated by a powerful concentration of thought. As it had been repeatedly stated in the preceding chapters any forms may be visualized through that process.

At that time I was camping near Punag ritöd in Kham. One afternoon, I was with my cook in a hut which we used as a kitchen. The boy asked me for some provisions. I answered, "Come with me to my tent, you can take what you need out of the boxes."

We walked out and when nearing my tent, we both saw the hermit lama seated on a folding chair next my camp table. This did not surprise us because the lama often came to talk

How To Read The Human Aura And Create An Intelligent Life Form

with me. The cook only said "Rimpoche is there, I must go and make tea for him at once, I will take the provisions later on."

I replied: "All right. Make tea and bring it to us."

The man turned back and I continued to walk straight toward the lama, looking at him all the time while he remained seated motionless. When I was only a few steps from the tent, a flimsy veil of mist seemed to open before it, like a curtain that is pulled aside. And suddenly I did not see the lama any more. He had vanished.

A little later, the cook came, bringing tea. He was surprised to see me alone. As I did not like to frighten him I said: "Rimpoche only wanted to give me a message. He had no time to stay to tea."

I related the vision to the lama, but he only laughed at me without answering my questions. Yet, upon another occasion he repeated the phenomenon. He utterly disappeared as I was speaking with him in the middle of a wide bare track of land, without tent or houses or any kind of shelter in the vicinity.

It is the custom in Tibet that the lamas who are initiated to that peculiar practice "put on" each morning the personality of their Yidam. This being done, the evil spirits who happen to meet these lamas do not see them as men, but under the frightful shape of the terrible deities; a sight which of course prevents them from attempting any mischief.

Expert magicians in this art can, it is said, hide their own real appearance under any illusory form they choose. Among the many who, each morning, gravely take on the shape of their Yidam, probably very few are really capable of showing themselves as such. I do not know if they succeed in duping the demons, but they certainly do not create any illusion to human eyes. Yet I have heard that some lamas have been seen in the appearance of certain deities of the lamaist pantheon.

Incited by many wonderful legends regarding the power of ancient tubthobs to create Tulpas, a small number of ngagspas and lamas endeavor, in great secrecy, to succeed in that peculiar branch of esoteric lore.

However, the practice is considered as fraught with danger for everyone who has not reached a high mental and spiritual degree of enlightenment and is not fully aware of the nature of the psychic forces at work in the process.

Once the Tulpa is endowed with enough vitality to be capable of playing the part of a real being, it tends to free itself from its maker's control. This, say Tibetan occultists, happens nearly mechanically, just as the child, when his body is completed and able to live apart, leaves its mother's womb. Sometimes the phantom becomes a rebellious son and one hears of uncanny struggles that have taken place between magicians and their creatures, the former being severely hurt or even killed by the latter.

Tibetan magicians also relate cases in which the Tulpa is sent to fulfill a mission, but does not come back and pursues its peregrinations as a half-conscious, dangerously mischievous puppet. The same thing, it is said, may happen when the maker of the Tulpa dies before having dissolved it. Yet, as a rule, the phantom either disappears suddenly at the death of the magician or gradually vanishes like a body that perishes for want of food.

On the other hand, some Tulpas are expressly intended to survive their creator and are specially formed for that purpose. These may be considered as veritable tulkus and, in fact, the demarcation between Tulpas and tulkus is far from being clearly drawn. The existence of both is grounded on the same theories.

Must we credit these strange accounts of rebellious "materializations," phantoms which have become real beings, or must we reject them all as mere fantastic tales and wild products of imagination? — Perhaps the latter course is the wisest. I affirm nothing. I only relate what I have heard from people whom, in other circumstances, I had found trustworthy, but they may have deluded themselves in all sincerity.

Nevertheless, allowing for a great deal of exaggeration and sensational addition, I could hardly deny the possibility of visualizing and animating a Tulpa. Besides having had few opportunities of seeing thought-forms, my habitual incredulity led me to make experiments for myself, and my efforts were attended with some success. In order to avoid being influenced by the forms of the lamaist deities, which I saw daily around me in paintings and images, I chose for my experiment a most insignificant character: a monk, short and fat, of an innocent and jolly type.

I shut myself in tsams and proceeded to perform the prescribed concentration of thought and other rites. After a few months the phantom monk was formed. His form grew gradually fixed and life-like looking. He became a kind of guest, living in my apartment. I then broke my seclusion and started for a tour, with my servants and tents.

The monk included himself in the party. Though I lived in the open riding on horseback for miles each day, the illusion persisted. I saw the fat trapa, now and then it was not necessary for me to think of him to make him appear. The phantom performed various actions of the kind that are natural to travelers and that I had not commanded. For instance, he walked, stopped, looked around him. The illusion was mostly visual, but sometimes I felt as if a robe was lightly rubbing against me and once a hand seemed to touch my shoulder.

The features which I had imagined, when building my phantom, gradually underwent a change. The fat, chubby-cheeked fellow grew leaner, his face assumed a vaguely mocking, sly, malignant look. He became more troublesome and bold. In brief, he escaped my control.

Once, a herdsman who brought me a present of butter saw the Tulpa in my tent and took it for a live lama.

I ought to have let the phenomenon follow its course, but the presence of that unwanted companion began to prove trying to my nerves; it turned into a "daynightmare." Moreover, I was beginning to plan my journey to Lhasa and needed a quiet brain devoid of other preoccupations, so I decided to dissolve the phantom. I succeeded, but only after six months of hard struggle. My mind-creature was tenacious of life.

There is nothing strange in the fact that I may have created my own hallucination. The interesting point is that in these cases of materialization, others see the thought forms that have been created.

Tibetans disagree in their explanations of such phenomena; some think a material form is really brought into being, others consider the apparition as a mere case of suggestion, the creator's thought impressing others and causing them to see what he himself sees.

Tulpas are able to think, and have their own free will, emotions, and memories. It takes time for a tulpa to develop a personality of their own; as they grow older, your attention and their life experiences will shape them into an entitie with their own hopes, dreams and beliefs.

CHAPTER VII
PSYCHIC INFLUENCE OF COLORS

IN all of Nature's wonderful processes we find many evidences of that great principle of Action and Reaction, which, like the forward and backward swing of the pendulum, changes cause into effect, and effect into cause, in a never ending series. We find this principle in effect in the psychic relation of mental states and colors. That is to say, that just as we find that certain mental and emotional states manifest in vibrations causing particular auric astral colors, so do we find that the presence of certain colors on the physical plane will have a decided psychic effect upon the mental and emotional states of individuals subject to their influence. And, as might be expected by the thoughtful student, the particular astral colors manifested in the aura by the presence of some particular mental or emotional state exactly correspond with the particular physical colors which influence that particular mental or emotional state.

Illustrating the statements in the preceding paragraph, I would say that the continued presence of red will be apt to set up emotional vibrations of anger, passion, physical love, etc., or, in a different tint, the higher physical emotions. Blue, of the right tint, will tend to cause feelings of spirituality, religious emotion, etc. Green is conducive to feelings of relaxation, repose, quiet, etc. Black produces the feeling of gloom and grief. And so on, each color tends to produce emotional vibrations similar to those which manifest that particular color in the astral aura of the person. It is a case of "give and take" along the entire scale of color and emotions, according to the great natural laws.

While the explanation of these facts is not known to the average person, nevertheless nearly everyone recognizes the subtle effect of color and avoids certain colors, while seeking certain others. There is not a single living human being but who has experienced the sense of rest, calm, repose, and calm inflow of strength, when in a room decorated in quiet shades of green. Nature, herself, has given this particular shade to the grass and leaves of trees and plants, so that the soothing effect of the country scene is produced. The aura of a person experiencing these feelings, and yielding to them, will manifest precisely the tint or shade of green which is shown on the grass and leaves around him, so true is this natural law of action and reaction.

The effect of scarlet upon animals, the bull for instance, is well known—to use the familiar term, it causes one to "see red." The sight of the color of blood is apt to arouse feelings of rage, or disgust, by reason of the same law. The sight of the beautiful clear blue sky tends to arouse feelings of reverence, awe or spirituality. One can never think of this shade of blue arousing rage; or red arouse feelings of spirituality.

It is a well known fact that in insane asylums, the use of red in decorations must be avoided, while the proper shades of blue or green are favored. On the other hand, the use of a proper red, in certain cases, will tend to arouse vitality and physical strength in a patient. It is not by mere chance that the life giving blood is a bright, rich red color when it leaves the heart.

When one "feels blue" he does not have the impression of a bright or soft blue--but he really is almost conscious of the presence of a dull bluish gray. And the presence of such a color in one's surroundings, tends to cause a feeling of depression. Everyone knows the effect of a "gray day" in the Fall or Spring.

Again, who does not know the feeling of mental exaltation coming from the sight of a day filled with golden sunshine, or from a golden sunset. We find proofs of this law of Nature on all sides, every day of our lives. It is an interesting subject, which will repay the student for the expenditure of a little time and thought upon it.

Speaking of the general class characteristics of the three primary groups of colors, all occultists, as well as many physiologists and psychologists, are agreed on the following fundamental propositions, viz.: that (1) Red is exciting to the mind and emotions; (2) Yellow is inspiring and elevating, and intellectually stimulating; and (3) Blue is cool, soothing, and calming. It is also universally conceded that the right shades of green (combining the qualities of blue and yellow in appropriate proportions) is the ideal color of rest and recuperation, followed by a stimulation and new ambition. The reason for this may be seen, when you consider the respective qualities of blue and yellow which compose this color.

It is interesting to note that the science of medicine is now seriously considering the use of colors in the treatment of disease, and the best medical authorities investigating the subject are verifying the teachings of the old occultists, regarding the influence of colors on mental states and physical conditions.

How To Read The Human Aura And Create An Intelligent Life Form

Dr. Edwin Babbitt, a pioneer in this line in the Western world, gave the general principles in a nutshell, when he laid down the following rule: "There is a trianal series of graduations in the peculiar potencies of colors, the center and climax of electrical action, which cools the nerves, being in violet; the climax of electrical action, which is soothing to the vascular system, being in blue; the climax of luminosity being in yellow; and the climax of thermism or heat being in red. This is not an imaginary division of qualities, but a real one, the flamelike red color having a principle of warmth in itself; the blue and violet, a principle of cold and electricity. Thus we have many styles of chromatic action, including progression of hues, of lights and shades, of fineness and coarseness, of electrical power, luminous power, thermal power, etc."

Read the above statement of Dr. Babbitt, and then compare it with the occult teaching regarding the astral colors, and you will perceive the real basis of the science which the good doctor sought to establish, and in which cause he did such excellent pioneer work. The result of his work is now being elaborated by modern physicians in the great schools of medicine, particularly on the Continent, in Europe--England and America being somewhat behind the times in this work.

The advanced occultist also finds much satisfaction in the interest, on the part of physicians and jurists, in the matter of the influence of color upon the mental, moral and physical welfare of the public. The effect of color upon morality is being noticed by workers for human welfare, occupying important offices.

The American journals report the case of a judge in a large Western city in that country, who insisted upon his courtroom being decorated in light, cheerful tints, instead of in the old, gloomy, depressing shades formerly employed. This judge wisely remarked that brightness led to right thinking, and darkness to crooked thinking; also that his court, being an uplift court, must have walls to correspond, and that it was enough to turn any man into a criminal to be compelled to sit in a dark, dismal courtroom, day after day.

This good judge, who must have had some acquaintance with the occult teachings, is quoted as concluding as follows: "White, cream, light yellow, and orange are the colors which are the sanest. I might add light green, for that is the predominant color in Nature; black, brown and deep red are incentives to crime--a man in anger sees red." Surely a remarkable utterance from the bench!

The effect of color schemes upon the moral and mental welfare of persons is being recognized in the direction of providing brighter color schemes in schools, hospitals, reformatories, prisons, etc. The reports naturally show the correctness of the underlying theory. The color of a tiny flower has its effect upon even the most hardened prisoner; while the minds of children in school are quickened by a touch of brightness here and there in the room. It needs no argument to prove the beneficial effect of the right kind of colors in the sickroom, or hospital ward.

The prevailing theories, and practice, regarding the employment of color in therapeutics and human welfare work, are in the main correct. But, I urge the study of the occult significance of color, as mentioned in this book in connection with the human aura and its astral colors, as a sound basis for an intelligent, thorough understanding of the real psychic principles underlying the physical application of the methods referred to. Go to the center of the subject, and then work outward--that is the true rule of the occultist, which might well be followed by the non-occult general public.

CHAPTER VIII
AURIC MAGNETISM

THE phenomenon of human magnetism is too well recognized by the general public, to require argument at this time. Let the scientist's dispute about it as much as they please, down in the heart of nearly all of the plain people of the race is the conviction that there is such a thing. The occultists, of course, are quite familiar with the wonderful manifestations of this great natural force, and with its effect upon the minds and bodies of members of the race, and can afford to smile at the attempts of some of the narrow minds in the colleges to pooh-pooh the matter.

But the average person is not familiar with the relation of this human magnetism to the human aura. I think that the student should familiarize himself with this fundamental relation, in order to reason correctly on the subject of human magnetism. Here is the fundamental fact in a nutshell: The human aura is the great storehouse, or reservoir, of human magnetism, and is the source of all human magnetism that is projected by the individual toward other individuals. Just how human magnetism is generated, is, of course, a far deeper matter, but it is enough for our purpose at this time to explain the fact of its storage and transmission.

In cases of magnetic healing, etc., the matter is comparatively simple. In such instances the healer by an effort of the will (sometimes unconsciously applied) projects a supply of his pranic aura vibrations into the body of his patient, by way of the nervous system of the patient, and also by means of what may be called the induction of the aura itself.

The mere presence of a person strongly charged with prana, is often enough to cause an overflow into the aura of other persons, with a resulting feeling of new strength and energy. By the use of the hands of the healer, a heightened effect is produced, by reason of certain properties inherent in the nervous system of both healer and patient.

There is even a flow of etheric substance from the aura of the healer to that of the patient, in cases where the vitality of the latter is very low. Many a healer has actually, and literally, pumped his life force and etheric substance into the body of his patient, when the latter was sinking into the weakness which precedes death, and has by so doing been able to bring him back to life and strength. This is practically akin to the transfusion of blood—except that it is on the psychic plane instead of the physical.

But the work of the magnetic healer does not stop here, if he be well informed regarding his science. The educated healer realizing the potent effect of mental states upon physical conditions--of mental vibrations upon the physical nerve centers and organs of the body—endeavors to arouse the proper mental vibrations in the mind of his patient. Ordinarily, he does this merely by holding in his mind the corresponding desired mental state, and thus arousing similar vibrations in the mind of the patient. This of itself is a powerful weapon of healing, and constitutes the essence of mental healing as usually practiced.

How To Read The Human Aura And Create An Intelligent Life Form

But there is a possible improvement even upon this, as we shall see in a moment.

The advanced occultist, realizing the law of action and reaction in the matter of the auric colors, turns the same to account in healing work, as follows: He not only holds in his mind the strong feeling and thought which he wishes to transmit to the patient, but (fix this in your mind) he also pictures in his imagination the particular kind of color which corresponds with the feeling or thought in question.

A moment's thought will show you that by this course he practically multiplies the effect. Not only do his own thought vibrations (1) set up corresponding vibrations in the mind of the patient, by the laws of thought transference, but (2) his thought of the certain colors will set up corresponding vibrations not only (a) in his own aura, and thence (b) to that of the patient, but will also (3) act directly upon the aura of the patient and reproduce the colors there, which (4) in turn will arouse corresponding vibrations in the mind of the patient, by the law of reaction.

The above may sound a little complicated at first reading, but a little analysis will show you that it is really quite a simple process, acting strictly along the lines of Action and Reaction, which law has been explained to you in preceding chapters of this book. The vibrations rebound from mind to aura, and from aura to mind, in the patient, something like a billiard ball flying from one side of the table to another, or a tennis ball flying between the two racquets over the net.

The principle herein mentioned may be employed as well in what is called "absent treatment" as in treatments where the patient is present. By the laws of thought transference, not only the thought but also the mental image of the appropriate astral color, is transmitted over space, and then, impinging on the mind of the patient, is transmitted into helpful and health-giving vibrations in his mind. The healer of any school of mental or spiritual healing will find this plan very helpful to him in giving absent as well as present treatments. I recommend it from years of personal experience, as well as that of other advanced occultists.

Of course the fact that the ordinary healer is not able to distinguish the finer shades of astral color, by reason of his not having actually perceived them manifested in the aura, renders his employment of this method less efficacious than that of the developed and trained occultist. But, nevertheless, he will find that, from the knowledge of the auric or astral colors given in this little book, he will be able to obtain quite satisfactory and marked results in his practice. The following table, committed to memory, will be of help to him in the matter of employing the mental image of the auric colors in his healing work.

TABLE OF HEALING COLORS.

Nervous System

Cooling and soothing: Shades of violet, lavender, etc.

Resting and invigorating effect: Grass greens.

Inspiring and illuminating: Medium yellows, and orange.

Stimulating and exciting: Reds (bright).

Blood and Organs

Cooling and soothing: Clear dark blues.

Resting and invigorating: Grass greens.

Inspiring and illuminating: Orange yellows.

Stimulating and exciting: Bright reds.

How To Read The Human Aura And Create An Intelligent Life Form

The following additional suggestions will be found helpful to the healer: In cases of impaired physical vitality; also chilliness, lack of bodily warmth, etc., bright, warm reds are indicated. In cases of feverishness, overheated blood, excessive blood pressure, inflammation, etc., blue is indicated. Red has a tendency to produce renewed and more active heart action; while violets and lavenders tend to slow down the too rapid beating of the heart. A nervous, unstrung patient may be treated by bathing her, mentally, in a flood of violet or lavender auric color; while a tired, used up, fatigued person may be invigorated by flooding him with bright reds, followed by bright, rich yellows, finishing the treatment with a steady flow of warm orange color.

To those who are sufficiently advanced in occult philosophy, I would say that they should remember the significance of the Great White Light, and accordingly conclude their treatment by an effort to indicate an approach to that clear, pure white color in the aura—mentally, of course. This will leave the patient in an inspired, exalted, illuminated state of mind and soul, which will be of great benefit to him, and will also have the effect of reinvigorating the healer by cosmic energy or para-prana.

Everything that has been said in this chapter regarding the use of color in magnetic treatments is equally applicable to cases of self-healing, or self-treatment. Let the patient follow the directions above given for the healer, and then turn the healing current, or thought, inward—and the result will be the same as if he were treating another. The individual will soon find that certain colors fit his requirements better than others, in which case let him follow such experience in preference to general rules, for the intuition generally is the safest guide in such cases.

CHAPTER IX

DEVELOPING THE AURA

WHEN it is remembered that the aura of the individual affects and influences other persons with whom he comes in contact--and is, in fact, an important part of his personality--it will be seen that it is important that the individual take pains to develop his aura in the direction of desirable qualities, and to neutralize and weed out undesirable ones. This becomes doubly true, when it is also remembered that, according to the law of action and reaction, the auric vibrations react upon the mind of the individual, thus intensifying and adding fuel to the original mental states which called them forth. From any point of view, it is seen to be an important part of self development and character building, to develop the aura according to scientific occult principles.

In this work of aura development, there is found to be two correlated phases, namely: (1) the direct work of flooding the aura with the best vibrations, by means of holding in the mind clear, distinct and repeated mental pictures of desirable ideas and feelings; and (2) the added effect of mental images of the colors corresponding to the ideas and feelings which are deemed desirable and worthy of development.

How To Read The Human Aura And Create An Intelligent Life Form

The first of the above mentioned phases is probably far more familiar to the average student, than is the second. This from the fact that the average student is apt to be more or less familiar with the teachings of the numerous schools or cults which agree in the axiom that "holding the thought" tends to develop the mind of the individual along the particular lines of such thought.

This is a correct psychological principle, for that matter, even when those practicing it do not fully understand the underlying facts. Mental faculties, like physical muscles, tend to develop by exercise and use, and any faculty may be developed and cultivated in this way.

Another teaching of these same schools is that the character of the thoughts so "held" by the individual, effects other persons with whom he comes in contact, and, in a way attracts to him objective things, persons, and circumstances in harmony with such thoughts. This also is in accordance with the best occult teaching--from which, of course, it was originally derived.

I heartily endorse the facts of these teachings, and pronounce them fundamentally correct. And, in this connection, I may say that every healer may apply his own methods PLUS this teaching regarding the aura, and thus obtain greatly increased results.

By the faithful, persevering, holding in mind of certain ideas and feelings, the individual may flood his aura with the vibrations and colors of such ideas and feelings, and thus charge it with auric energy and power. By so doing, he gains the benefit of the reaction upon his own mind, and also secures the advantage of the effect thereof upon other persons with whom he comes in contact. In this way he not only builds up his individual character along desirable lines, but at the same time develops a strong, positive, attractive "personality" which affects others with whom he comes in contact.

I do not consider it necessary to go into details here regarding this phase of "holding the thought," for, as I have said, the average student is already familiar with the rules regarding the same. In a nutshell, however, I will say that each individual is largely the result of the thoughts he has manifested, and the feelings which he has harbored. Therefore, the rule is to manifest and exercise the faculties you would develop, and inhibit or refrain from manifesting the ones you would restrain or control. Again, to restrain an undesirable faculty, develop and exercise its opposite--kill out the negatives by developing the positives. The mind produces thought; and yet, it tends to grow from the particular portion of its own product which you may choose to feed to it--for it not only creates thought, but also feeds upon it. So, finally, let it produce the best kind of thought for you, and then throw that back into the hopper, for it will use it to grind out more of the same kind and grow strong in so doing. That is the whole thing in a nutshell.

The second phase of aura development (as above classified), however, is not likely to be familiar to the average student, for the reason that it is not known outside of advanced occult circles, and very little has been allowed to be taught regarding it. But, the very reticence regarding it is a proof of its importance, and I strongly advise my students to give to it the attention and practice that its importance merits. The practice, thereof, however, is extremely simple, and the principle of the practice, moreover, is based solely upon the facts of the relation of color and mental states, as shown in the astral auric colors, as fully explained in the preceding chapters of this book.

How To Read The Human Aura And Create An Intelligent Life Form

In order to intelligently practice the development of the aura by means of flooding or charging it with the vibrations of psychic colors, it is first necessary that the student be thoroughly familiar with the scale of colors related to each set of mental states or emotional feelings. This scale and its key is found in a number of places in the preceding chapters.

The student should turn back the pages of this book, and then carefully re-read and re-study every word which has been said about the relation of mental states and auric colors. He should know the mental correspondence of the shades of red, yellow, and blue, so thoroughly that the thought of one will bring the idea of the other. He should be able to think of the corresponding group of colors, the moment he thinks of any particular mental state. He should be thoroughly familiar with the physical, mental, and spiritual effect of any of the colors, and should moreover, test himself, psychically, for the individual effects of certain colors upon himself.

He should enter into this study with interest and earnestness, and then by keeping his eyes and ears open, he will perceive interesting facts concerning the subject on every side in his daily work and life. He will perceive many proofs of the principle, and will soon amass a stock of experiences illustrating each color and its corresponding mental state. He will be richly repaid for the work of such study, which, in fact, will soon grow to be more like pleasure than like work.

Having mastered this phase of the subject, the student should give himself a thorough, honest, self-examination and mental analysis. He should write down a chart of his strong points and his weak ones. He should check off the traits which should be developed, and those which should be restrained. He should determine whether he needs development along physical, mental, and spiritual lines, and in what degree.

Having made this chart of himself, he should then apply the principles of charging the aura with the color vibrations indicated by his self diagnosis and prescription.

The last stage is quite simple, once one has acquired the general idea back of it. It consists simply in forming as clear a mental image as possible of the color or colors desired, and then projecting the vibrations into the aura by the simple effort of the will. This does not mean that one needs to clinch the fist or frown the brow, in willing. Willing, in the occult sense, may be said to consist of a COMMAND, leaving the rest to the mechanism of the will and mind. Take away the obstacle of Doubt and Fear—then the Royal Command performs the work of setting the will into operation. This, by the way, is an important occult secret, of wide application, try to master its all important significance.

The mental imaging of colors may be materially aided by concentration upon physical material of the right color. By concentrating the attention and vision upon a red flower, for instance; or upon a bit of green leaf, in another instance; one may be able to form a clear, positive mental image of that particular color. This accompanied by the willing, and demand, that the vibrations of this color shall charge the aura, will be found to accomplish the result. Have something around you showing the desirable colors, and your attention will almost instinctively take up the impression thereof, even though you may be thinking of, or doing something else. Live as much as possible in the idea and presence of the desirable color, and you will get the habit of setting up the mental image and vibration thereof. A little practice and experience will soon give you the idea, and enable you to get the best results. Patience, perseverance, and sustained earnest interest--that is the key of success.

CHAPTER X
THE PROTECTIVE AURA

AMONG the very oldest of the teachings of occultism, we find instructions regarding the building up and maintenance of the protective aura of the individual, whereby he renders himself immune to undesirable physical, mental, psychic or spiritual influences. So important is this teaching, that it is to be regretted that there has not been more said on the subject by some of the writers of recent years. The trouble with many of these recent writers is that they seem to wish to close their eyes to the unpleasant facts of life, and to gaze only upon the pleasant ones. But this is a mistake, for ignorance has never been a virtue, and to shut one's eyes to unpleasant facts does not always result in destroying them. I consider any teaching unfinished and inadequate which does not include instruction along protective lines.

Physical auric protection consists in charging the aura with vital magnetism and color, which will tend to ward off not only the physical contagion of ill persons, but, what is often still more important, the contagion of their mind and feelings.

The student who has really studied the preceding chapters will at once realize that this protection is afforded by filling the aura with the vibrations of health and physical strength, by means of the mental imaging of the life-preserving reds, and the exercise of the mind in the direction of thought of strength and power. These two things will tend to greatly increase the resistive aura of anyone, and enable him to throw off disease influences which affect others.

The aura of the successful physician and healer, in the presence of disease, will invariably show the presence of the bright, positive red in the aura, accompanied by the mental vibrations of strength, power and confidence, and the absence of fear. This in connection with the Auric Circle, which shall be described presently, will be of great value to healers, physicians, nurses, etc., as well as to those who are brought into intimate contact with sick persons.

Of practically the same degree of importance, is the charging of the aura with the vibrations of mental protection, viz, the vibrations of orange, yellow and similar colors. These are the colors of intellect, you will remember, and when the aura is charged and flooded with them it acts as a protection against the efforts of others to convince one against his will, by sophistical arguments, plausible reasoning, fallacious illustrations, etc. It gives to one a sort of mental illumination, quickening the perceptive faculties, and brightening up the reasoning and judging powers, and finally, giving a sharp edge to the powers of repartee and answer.

If you will assume the right positive mental attitude, and will flood your aura with the vibrations of the mental orange-yellow, the mental efforts of other persons will rebound from your aura, or, to use another figure of speech, will slip from it like water from the back of the proverbial duck. It is well to carry the mental image of your head being surrounded by a golden aura or halo, at such times--this will be found especially efficacious as a protective helmet when you are assaulted by the intellect or arguments of others.

And, again, there is a third form of protective aura, namely protection of one's emotional nature--and this is highly important, when one remembers how frequently we are moved to action by our emotions, rather than by our intellect or reason. To guard one's emotions, is to guard one's very inmost soul, so to speak. If we can protect our feeling and emotional side, we will be able to use our reasoning powers and intellect far more effectively, as all know by experience.

What color should we use in this form of auric protection? Can anyone be in doubt here, if he has read the preceding chapters? What is the emotional protective color – why, blue, of course. Blue controls this part of the mind or soul, and by raising ourselves into the vibrations of positive blue, we leave behind us the lower emotions and feelings, and are transported into the higher realms of the soul where these low vibrations and influences cannot follow us. In the same way, the blue colored aura will act as an armor to protect us from the contagion of the low passions and feelings of others.

If you are subjected to evil influences, or contagion of those harboring low emotions and desires, you will do well to acquire the art of flooding your aura with the positive blue tints. Make a study of bright, clear blues, and you will instinctively select the one best suited for your needs. Nature gives us this instinctive knowledge, if we will but seek for it, and then apply it when found. The aura of great moral teachers, great priests and preachers, advanced occultists, in fact all men of lofty ideals working among those lower on the moral scale, are always found to be charged with a beautiful, clear blue, which acts as a protection to them when they are unduly exposed to moral or emotional contagion. Ignorance of the occult laws have caused the downfall of many a great moral teacher, who could have protected himself in this way, in times of strong attack of low vibrations, had he but known the truth. The individual who knows this law, and who applies it, is rendered absolutely immune from evil contagion on the emotional plane of being.

The Great Auric Circle

But no occult instruction on this subject would be complete without a reference to the Great Auric Circle of Protection, which is a shelter to the soul, mind, and body, against outside psychic influences, directed, consciously or unconsciously against the individual. In these days of wide spread though imperfect, knowledge of psychic phenomena, it is especially important that one should be informed as to this great shield of protection. Omitting all reference to the philosophy underlying it, it may be said that this Auric Circle is formed by making the mental image, accompanied by the demand of will, of the aura being surrounded by a great band of PURE CLEAR WHITE LIGHT. A little perseverance will enable you to create this on the astral plane, and, though (unless you have the astral vision) you cannot see it actually, yet you will actually FEEL its protective presence, so that you will know that it is there guarding you.

This White Auric Circle will be an effective and infallible armor against all forms of psychic attack or influence, no matter from whom it may emanate, or whether directed consciously or unconsciously. It is a perfect and absolute protection, and the knowledge of its protective power should be sufficient to drive fear from the heart of all who have dreaded psychic influence, "malicious animal magnetism" (so-called), or anything else of the kind, by whatever name known. It is also a protection against psychic vampirism, or draining of magnetic strength.

The Auric Circle is, of course, really egg-shaped, or oval, for it fringes the aura as the shell cases the egg. See yourself, mentally, as surrounded by this Great White Auric Circle of Protection, and let the idea sink into your consciousness. Realize its power over the influences from outside, and rejoice in the immunity it gives you.

The Auric Circle, however, will admit any outside impressions that you really desire to come to you, while shutting out the others. That is, with this exception, that if your inner soul recognizes that some of these desired influences and impressions are apt to harm you (though your reason and feeling know it not) then will such impressions be denied admittance. For the White Light is the radiation of Spirit, which is higher than ordinary mind, emotion, or body and is Master of All. And its power, even though we can but imperfectly represent it even mentally, is such that before its energy, and in its presence, in the aura, all lower vibrations are neutralized and disintegrated.

The highest and deepest occult teaching is that the White Light must never be used for purpose of attack or personal gain, but that it may properly be used by anyone, at any time, to protect against outside psychic influences against which the soul protests. It is the armor of the soul, and may well be employed whenever or wherever the need arises.

Throughout the pages of this little book have been scattered crumbs of teaching other than those concerning the aura alone. Those for whom these are intended will recognize and appropriate them—the others will not see them, and will

How To Read The Human Aura And Create An Intelligent Life Form

pass them by. One attracts his own to him. Much seed must fall on waste places, in order that here and there a grain will find lodgment in rich soil awaiting its coming. True occult knowledge is practical power and strength. Beware of prostituting the higher teachings for selfish ends and ignoble purposes. To guard and preserve your own will is right; to seek to impose your will upon that of another is wrong. Passive resistance is often the strongest form of resistance—this is quite different from non-resistance.

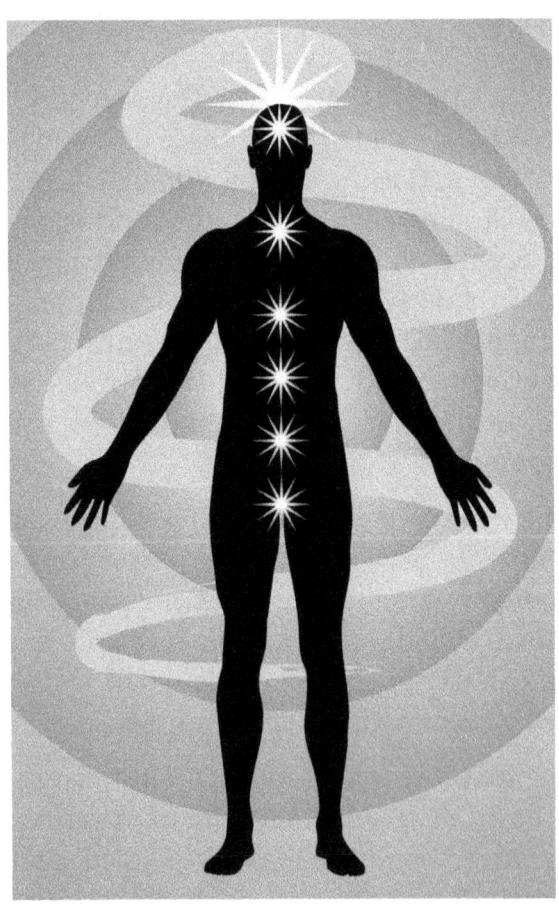

How To Read The Human Aura And Create An Intelligent Life Form

CHAPTER XI
COLOR VIBRATIONS

IN his book "*YOU*," author Charles F Haanel writes that all force, all matter, all energy – even your life itself – is a vibratory activity that conforms to precise natural laws. So if you really want to understand how to create Tulpas, how and why the human aura acts the way it doew, and why the universe is the way it is, you must come to an understanding of how vibrations operate and manifest.

The varying velocities of light contain all the splendors of the universe. The velocities decrease from white light (186,000 miles a second) through violet, indigo, blue, green, yellow, orange, and red to black (140,000 miles a second). It is by the varying movements of these velocities that the eye is affected by the sensation known as color.

The molecular constitution of a body determines the character and speed of the light vibrations it returns to the eye, and thus gives each body its own characteristic color. Hence, the term "color" is used to denote the different appearances that matter presents to the eye independent of its form.

Black is composed of equal parts of red, yellow, and blue. White is composed of five parts of red, three parts of yellow, and eight parts of blue. Normal or natural gray is composed of white and black in equal proportions. Black, therefore, means the result of all colors, while white signifies the reflection of all colors; and each color in its turn is but a mode of motion, or the varying sensations that we experience when these vibrations impinge upon the optic nerve.

Color is, therefore, one of the manifestations of vibration and all vibration manifests in corresponding color, the color being merely an indication of the occult chemical activity.

The color indicates not only the quality but the value of any chemical substance by reason of its own particular rate of vibration, and all objects of any particular color have that vibratory activity and vibratory value which pertain to that color. As the color is, so is the vibration.

Nature's scale of vibration is very wide in its extent. It commences with sound, then merges into thermal heat waves, and these vibrations climb the vibratory scale as the temperature increases and merge into the vibrations of the radiant heat waves in the infrared which reach up to the visible red of the light spectrum.

The vibrations above the infrared are:

Visible Red - 15 trillions

Orange - 20 trillions

Yellow - 28 trillions

Green - 35 trillions

Blue - 50 trillions

Indigo - 60 trillions

Violet - 75 trillions

How To Read The Human Aura And Create An Intelligent Life Form

The sensation of color, therefore, depends on the number of vibrations of light ether, just as the pitch of a note depends on the number of vibrations of the sounding body. The number of vibrations for each color is constant. These seven different rates of vibration that we know as colors make up the visible light spectrum. Beyond these are series of vibrations known as the ultra-violet. These extend up to those vibrations designated as radioactivity, of which radium and the X-rays are best known examples. This ends both the light spectrum and natures vibratory scales so far as present knowledge goes. As the quality and value of all forms of energy are due to their rates of vibration, it follows that color will indicate the quality of the vibrating energy.

Color, like the diatonic scale, is divided into seven distinct notes.

Red has a stimulating effect. The disturbing influence of red is well illustrated by the expression "painting the town red," indicating recklessness and destruction.

Yellow is a nerve tonic. It is the climax of luminosity, and symbolizes sunlight itself. It produces the feeling of joy and gaiety.

Green has a quieting and soothing effect. It is the color of nature and suggests life. It checks mental activity and suggests sleep.

Blue suggests space, vastness. It is depressing and chilling. One who is continually in a blue environment will sooner or later have the "blues." It is a melancholy color.

Violet is magnetic and cooling.

Each color has a distinct frequency or vibration due to wavelengths. Red has a larger wave length than blue, which is proportionately much shorter. That is why the quick notes of the drums arouse the emotions of the savage—they express in sound what red expresses in color, while the neutral notes of the flute or horn have a quieting influence. They express in sound what blue expresses in color.

These manifestations are recognized as they are perceived by the different nerves, for the mind of man translates the impressions of the world into facts of consciousness and thought by means of the nerves. All these varying rates of vibration differ only in direction, rate, and frequency, and are interpreted according to the different nerves or groups of nerves physically attuned to them or organized to select and respond to especial manifestations of vibratory activity.

Color is both physical and psychological in its effect upon the mind. The physical effect is a chemical one; the psychological effect is psychic. The nervous system reflects its disturbances upon the mind; hence the sensation of pain or pleasure and the emotional states that accompany them. This is true of all the colors. Primary colors are radical, elemental, and fixed in their vibrations or wave lengths, and hence, when once the effects of the sensations which they produce on the mind are known, their uniformity can always be depended upon.

Red is thermal and a stimulant and blue is electrical and depressing. They act uniformly on all forms of life. The spectrum analysis proves that the seven colors of light are made up of vibrations or wave lengths of mathematical exactness.

As all vibratory activity expresses itself in form, color, and sound, it follows that the energy is always of that particular color, shade, or tint that belongs to that particular rate of vibration. This is true not only of those colors, shades, and tints that are perceptible to visible light, but also of the finer forces of nature that transcend the physical senses.

All energy of whatever quality is continually vibrating and, by reason of this vibration, it assumes the color, shade, or tint belonging to that specific rate of vibration.

The primary colors are red, blue, and yellow. All the other colors are combinations of these colors in certain proportions, red is the physical color and is the color of all physical energy. The various shades of red have their various significations, but, generally speaking, red is the physical color.

Red is also the color of the will. Where ever the will is expressed, it assumes the red color because Will is the outflowing or manifesting principle, the extension or expression of the self into manifestation. Therefore it must express itself in and through the physical; consequently, it becomes red in color.

The second primary color is blue, the color of emotion. All energy vibrating on the higher octave is either blue or red according as it is positive or negative—blue being the negative, feminine, or magnetic side of matter and red the positive, masculine, or radiant side. The bluer the matter may be, the more magnetic it is, while the redder it may be the more electrical it is. Will and Desire are thus the two poles of etheric matter—Will being red, Desire being blue.

The third primary color is yellow and it is the color of the mental plane. Everything vibrating on the mental octave is yellow. The darker the yellow, the more gross and material is the character of the thought; the lighter it becomes, the more spiritual it is. The clearer the yellow is, the more purity of thought. The brighter the yellow, the more brilliancy of mind is indicated.

How To Read The Human Aura And Create An Intelligent Life Form

Yellow or orange symbolize the highest function and power of our nature and preeminently typify the "scientific" temperament.

White is really the combination of all the seven colors. They are all found to unite in forming the white ray. The prism has the power of breaking up the white light into seven prismatic rays, therefore white light is really the combination of those rays.

Pure white is unity. It is in fact the very essence of balance. It is the star of hope that typifies cleanliness and symbolizes power. It is the language of knowledge, expression, and spirituality.

Virgin white not only signifies cleanliness, but purity and naturally, the mind is consciously as well as unconsciously affected by it.

Black is the reverse of white. White indicates the spirit. Black indicates extreme materiality; not materiality in the sense of physical substance, but materiality as the antithesis of spirit. Black indicates the disintegration which leads to annihilation.

Black is repressing, depressing, and suppressing. It represents the negative conditions of gloom, fear, error, disease, ignorance, pessimism, and hopelessness.

Black typifies the universal negative in which all color is hid, absorbed, and is emblematic of death, oblivion, and annihilation.

Scarlet is the color of anger, the color which the astral body assumes when it is in an intensely angry condition. Anger is really the forcible action of the will moving outward in a very positive manner. This is what produces the state of anger.

How To Read The Human Aura And Create An Intelligent Life Form

The color of ether is pink, although its vibration is so intense that very few are able to see the vibration; but ether is always pink. Crimson is the color of affection and human feeling. It is the self-relative color, because our affection is given to persons on account of their particular relation to us.

Affection is purely a physical and animal feeling.

Rose is the color of life, and as we approach the physical it is more red. As life is brought under the influence of the emotions, it takes on whatever color is found, blended with this red or rose color.

Indigo blue is the color of occultism. The dark indigo partakes of the element of screen, while the pure indigo is emblematic of pure occultism.

Violet is the color of magic because it is so far above the ordinary rate of vibration that it has the power of neutralizing and even transforming those rates into its own, thus giving the power of alchemy.

Purple being blue mixed with red, the positive aspect of emotion, is the color of mastership, and indicates the master.

Lavender, which is a great deal of white mixed with purple, indicates the master on the astral plane, but merging toward the spiritual.

Green is the color of action. It is expressed by minor chords, and is the positive expression of the inner being as expressed through action.

Unselfish action—action which is purely altruistic in its character, which has no relation whatever to the individual—is a clear emerald green, and the nearer this approaches to the spiritual the paler it becomes.

Brown is, in a sense, a mystical color, in that it indicates the presence of white, red, and black in certain combinations. As the shade is, so will its influence be.

As all the colors are included in the white, so is all matter built up of simpler or elemental substances and all changes are due to distribution and aggregation of the elemental matter.

Motion is the primary cause that gives rise to color and all other phenomena in existence. In order to trace the origin and progress of any effect, visible or invisible, the aim must be to determine the movement or movements which brought the phenomena into existence.

The principle of vibration permeates the whole science of radiation or motion and may be stated in a general way by saying that a body absorbs waves that are of the same period as those which it emits when it is itself in vibration.

The essential condition is therefore that the receiver shall be in the same key or wave length as the sender or origin of the movement. The original wave gives energy to the wave upon which it impinges. While one is gaining energy, the other is losing it and this continues until the process of absorption is completed.

This principle applies to light, heat, sound, color, or energy of any kind, where it is distributed by a process of radiation.

Cosmic Vibrations

With color vibrations and the human aura, we must also consider the significance of other forms of vibrations and how they influence us. Most of us are unaware to the wonderful truth outlined in the sky—truths more wonderful, more glorious than any tale of mystery or romance, truths that are continually spread before us in Nature's great book.

The Greeks mapped out the geography of the heavens that is now used more than 1,400 years before Christ. Ptolemy recorded no less than forty-eight of the largest and best known constellations of stars, more than 600 years previous to this, and remember that the telescope was invented only 400 years ago.

Our painted American savages, the Arab in the desert, the simple children on the banks of the Nile, the wild men of the islands of the sea have all been more observant of the mystery hid in the stars than we as a people are today.

The solar system, from the highest spiritual point down to the lowest physical, is one vast organized whole, nowhere dead, nowhere unconscious, nowhere useless, nowhere accidental; but carefully gathered, ordered, and supervised to express the indwelling life and intelligence of its Creator and to subserve His plans. In fact, it is one gigantic Being, throbbing with vitality and consciousness.

The distance of stars from us is so great that it conveys no impression on the mind to state them in miles; some other method, therefore, must be used, and the velocity of light affords us a convenient one. Light travels at the rate of 186,000 miles a second, and by using this as a measuring rod, we can form a better idea of the distance of stars. Thus, the nearest star, Alpha Centauri, is situated at a distance which light requires three and a half years to traverse.

On the average, light requires fifteen and a half years to reach us from a star of the second magnitude, forty-three years from a star of the third, and so on, until, for stars of the twelfth magnitude, the time required is 3,500 years.

How To Read The Human Aura And Create An Intelligent Life Form

How have astronomers ascertained that the star nearest to our solar system is twenty-five trillion miles away? The diameter of the Earth's orbit is 186,000,000 miles; that is to say, that in six months from today, the Earth will be on the other side of the Sun and therefore 186,000,000 miles away from its present position. Now, if we photograph the stars today and six months from now we photograph them again, the second photograph will show that some of the stars have shifted their position ever so slightly with regard to all the rest of the stars.

The reason for this shift is easily understood by comparing the stars to a line of lanterns at night. If you stand just a little way off from that line, you will see the lanterns as so many points of light all close together; but if you walk off at right angles for a little distance, you will see them somewhat separated from each other and the nearest ones will appear to be separated from each other more than the farthest ones. This is termed parallax.

The Earth in altering its position by 186,000,000 shows us parallax which, for the nearest stars, are great enough for the astronomer to use in calculating their distances. If he can measure the parallax of a star, it is then a slight matter to calculate the distance of that star from the Earth.

The telescope on Mount Wilson, California, is 100 inches in diameter; it took seven years to grind the disk, which is coated with silver. The disk alone weighs four and one-half tons. It does not magnify as is commonly supposed, but simply gathers the light and brings it to a focus. In this case, the reflection is 250,000 times that of the human eye and enables us to penetrate 400 times further into space.

How To Read The Human Aura And Create An Intelligent Life Form

Any magnification maybe used in the eye piece, a magnification power of from 3,000 to 6,000 is generally used in viewing the planets. A great clockwork motor is used to counteract the apparent motion of the heavens caused by the rotation of the Earth. The movement of this motor is so accurate that a star will remain in the same point in the eye piece as long as may be desired.

The Sun and his family of planets revolve around a central sun, which is millions of miles distant. It requires something less than 26,000 years to make one revolution. His orbit is called the Zodiac, which is divided into twelve signs, familiarly known as Aries, Taurus, Gemini, Cancer, Leo, Virgo, Libra, Scorpio, Sagittarius, Capricorn, Aquarius, and Pisces.

It requires our Solar System a little more than 2,100 years to pass through one of these signs, and this time is the measurement of an Age or Dispensation. Because of what astronomers call "the precession of the Equinoxes," the movement of the Sun through the signs of the Zodiac is in order reverse from that given above.

For some years past, the Solar System, which includes our planet Earth, has been entering the Zodiacal sign Aquarius. An airy, mental, electrical sign, which inclines to metaphysical, psychological, progressive, and changed conditions; cooperative and equalizing in its influence. It conduces to investigation, interest in serial matters, means of transit, means of communication, of education, of hygiene, and of new forms of government.

Its planetary ruler is Uranus, called "The Reformer," who destroys but to rebuild better anew. It is Uranus that "makes old things pass away, that all things may become new." It conduces to liberty, freedom, and expression. It has been called the human sign.

The twelve signs are alternately positive and negative in their nature—each contains a certain specialized influence of its own, having a ruler from which the nature of its influence is obtained. The Sun radiates energy to every member of its solar family. As the central figure among the planets, its position indicates the sphere of activity in which the individual will meet with greatest success and is the essential impulse and driving force that urges him to do it.

The Sun is the ruler of all life, the Moon is the giver of all form, and as life manifests through form, the relationship of the Sun and Moon is inseparable, and it becomes the task of everyone to subject the Moon or form side of his existence to the Sun or life side, and the degree of success that he attains in doing this will be the measure of his ability to rule his stars.

As the Sun is the Life-giver of the Solar System and the heart is the Life-giver of the Body, it is easy to see why the Sun's influence is the greatest in the nativity of Man, as it operates directly through the heart.

The influence of the Moon is greatest in the first half of life, and the influence of the Sun is the greatest in the second half. Every planet has definite characteristics that impress themselves upon the child at birth. This is due to the electrostatic condition of the atmosphere at the time of the child's first inspiration of air, by which a vital change takes place in the nature of the blood. For this reason, those who are born under the influence of a particular planet portray the characteristics of that planet most strongly in their mental temperament, and this finds reflection in both motive and action.

How To Read The Human Aura And Create An Intelligent Life Form

In addition to the influence of particular planets, there is the influence of the various constellations. They are usually divided into Cardinal, Fixed, and Mutable signs.

The cardinal will make the character acute, active, restless, aspiring, and changeable. The mutable, indifferent, slow, vacillating, and hesitating; yet tractable and impressionable. The fixed will make it determined, decisive, firm, ambitious, and unbending; slow to move, yet irresistible when started.

The constellations easily fall into the following divisions:

Cardinal: Aries—Cancer—Libra—Capricorn

Fixed: Taurus—Leo—Scorpio—Aquarius

Mutable: Gemini—Virgo—Sagittarius—Pisces

The influence of the cardinal-sign is to stir the latent forces into action, promote change, and create initiative.

The influence of the fixed-sign is for stability. The individual may be slow and plodding, but he will be persistent; he will know no defeat; he will concentrate upon one point and pursue it to the end; his seal will be almost fanatical.

The influence of the mutable-sign is flexibility and change. This influence is purely mental or spiritual and gives purpose and incentive to action.

The cardinal type, therefore, is active; the mutable type restless; and the fixed type rigid. As material success depends upon action, the important factors in the world's work are derived from this type.

How To Read The Human Aura And Create An Intelligent Life Form

As stability is a necessary factor in important industrial undertakings, the fixed type frequently share the material and financial success with the cardinal type. The mutable type is, however, adverse to effort—they want adventure, change, travel; they are therefore the promoters who bring manufacturer and inventor together; they are the vendors and middlemen and the agents who negotiate between buyer and seller.

They are also the sensitives, and react more keenly to the experiences of life; they carry the heavier burden because they feel more. They participate in the issues of life to a greater degree because they carry not only their own burden, but the burdens of those around them. The greater possibilities of inner unfoldment, understanding, and development are always with the sensitive. The sensitive uses not only reason, but imagination, vision, intuition, and insight.

The fixed types are usually the materialists who are content with objective possessions and attainments. They use their reason and are interested in that only which can be measured or can be seen, felt, and handled. They are the doers rather than the dreamers and are utterly stable; they fill many responsible positions with great success, and are valuable members of society.

Neither type is superior, they are simply different—both are necessary.

The fixed signs represent something ingathered, collected together, accumulated, and relatively unified; something definite and uniform; a center of power and possibility, relatively quiescent and unchanging in itself receiving from outside and giving back again when required. They resemble violent explosives, which are inert while they are undisturbed, but contain large stores of energy locked up within them, and produce sudden and violent effects when stimulated to liberate it. The cardinal signs are always on the surface, never inert, never still, full of activity, ever busy and changing—they attract the most attention in the world.

The mutable signs are intermediate between the two extremes, fluctuate between them, and can ally themselves with either; but they are never so steadfast as the one nor so active and open as the other. In accordance with this, it may be noted that three out of the four mutable signs are described as "double."

In terms of character as applied to the average age man of today, fixed signs indicate persons in whom feeling, desire, or emotion is strong in one or more of the many forms this phase of consciousness can assume. It may be selfish or unselfish according to the impression given their being at the moment of birth by the planetary vibrations prevailing at that time and place.

Such persons are averse to change and have settled views and habits that are very difficult to alter whether good or bad. They vary from the patient and enduring to the obstinate and determined. They sometimes follow one occupation or way of life for a longtime without a change. They make faithful friends and unrelenting enemies.

Cardinal signs signify persons who are full of activity, either of body or mind, often of both. They are restless, busy, venturesome, daring, bold, can cut out paths in life for themselves; are innovators, pioneers, abandoning the old and seeking after the new. They are self-reliant and ambitious; often make noticeable, popular, or notorious figures in their sphere of life; may be found occupying public positions, or exercising authority over others. They are generous and impulsive, move and act quickly. They have not the plodding perseverance of the fixed signs, but can work hard and quickly, and achieve much in a short time. They seek rather to mold circumstances to their will than to adapt themselves to circumstances as do natives of mutable signs, or to overcome by dogged persistence as the fixed signs can. They are quick both to love and hate, easily make both friends and enemies, but their feelings may change as quickly. Activity is the keynote of their character, no matter in what channel it may run, whether practical, emotional, or intellectual—and whether for good or evil.

Mutable signs are more difficult to delineate. Adaptability may perhaps express their meaning. In the practical affairs of life, the natives of these signs show neither the activity that molds circumstances to their will (characteristic of cardinal signs) nor the perseverance and endurance of the fixed signs; but rather seek to gain their ends by adapting themselves to circumstances by intelligent discrimination and the avoidance of extremes. They take the circuitous path when the direct road is not open, and sometimes even when it is open. This tendency shows itself in a great variety of ways. They can adapt themselves to the habits and moods of other people, they can easily see both sides of a question, and can honestly sympathize with quite contradictory opinions and principles. In the sphere of the emotions, this may make them sympathetic, humane, and charitable, and lovers of peace and quietness. Intellectually, it may give a very impartial, subtle, penetrating, and discriminating mind. They are to some extent natural managers, messengers, travelers, or intermediaries, in a general sense; interpret or express the feelings and ideas of others, make writers and speakers of all grades, from clerk to author, from lawyer to preacher. In the individuality, the cardinal signs give executive ability and action that is unifying in nature and in accordance with divine law; the mutable signs cognize likenesses, synthesis, and draw together; and the fixed signs give stability and realization of the unity underlying apparent separateness.

These signs may be further differentiated as follows:

Earthy—Practical and material, commercial, intellectual, and scientific.

Watery—Emotional and plastic, sympathetic and resolvent; reproductive.

Airy—Refined and artistic, given to abstract ideas.

Fiery—Spiritual and idealistic, energizing and creative.

They are defined as follows:

Earthy: Taurus—Virgo—Capricorn

Fiery: Aries—Leo—Sagittarius

Airy: Gemini—Libra—Aquarius

Watery: Cancer—Scorpio—Pisces

Earth is the lowest and outermost of the states of matter: the most differentiated, limited, and complex: and the farthest removed from the state of pure spirit. In its reference to a cosmic plane, it signifies the physical plane; as a state of matter, it means the solid; in reference to man, it means the physical body; as a state of consciousness, it represents action, doing, volition as distinguished from feeling or thinking.

Persons in whose nativity the Earth is predominant show as many modifications and classes as do natives of other elements; but they are generally practical, matter-of-fact people of the world who are better at doing than at thinking or feeling;

or who try to reduce thought and emotion to practical applications.

They may be said to be natural executants, but their service varies from that of the prime clerk, the shop assistant, and the laborer; and they range from the wise to the foolish, from the actively ambitious, selfish, or unselfish to the passive, inert, and unenterprising.

Water, as a state of matter, means the liquid state. In its application to a cosmic plane, it signifies the next interior one to the physical, called variously the astral or psychic plane. It expresses consciousness through feelings, emotions, desires, instincts, passions, intuitions; and those who are born under it show both the strength and the weakness of this side of human nature. They vary from the sympathetic, affectionate, charitable, imaginative, sincere, and religious to the indolent, luxury-loving, passionate, selfish, listless, and inert.

Air, as a state of matter, means the gaseous state. It corresponds to sunset and expresses consciousness through thought and understanding. Those who are born under airy signs show many and various gradations of intellect, from the literary to the scientific, from the metaphysical to the poetic, from the busy, practical, and executive to the profound, comprehensive, and solid. The imagination, whether expressed through poetry, music, or art, seems to belong partly to the air and partly to either fire or water.

Fire corresponds to sunrise and to individualization. People coming under fire signs are impulsive, energetic, enthusiastic, positive, impetuous, and active. They seem to resemble the natives of watery signs more than those of earth or air, for they live more in the feelings, emotions, and passions than in the intellect. In so far as it is represented by the Sun, fire may stand for the energizing and all-permeating life of the Universe everywhere, the main-spring of all evolution—all progress.

This, then, is the laboratory in which Nature is forever combining the spiritual forces that result in the infinite diversity on every side, for "All are parts of one stupendous whole." Energy is a mode of motion, and we are conscious of motion by its effect only. This effect, if transmitted to the brain through the vehicle of the eye, makes itself known as light; if it impinges upon the ear, we know it as sound.

Whether this energy shall reach the eye or the ear depends upon the length and frequency of the vibrations.

Radio waves vibrate from 10,000 to 30,000,000 times a second; heat and light waves much faster. Radio waves are therefore extremely long, heat waves shorter, and light waves still shorter.

The length of a wave depends upon its frequency, that is, the number of waves which pass a given point in one second.

We may compare electrical or radio waves to the bass note of a musical scale. As we go up the scale, the waves become shorter and shorter and the frequency higher and higher, until they produce the sensation of heat. If the frequency is increased, visible light waves will appear.

As the frequency is increased, the sensation of light is finally lost; here we contact the ultraviolet or X-ray. As it still further increases, we no longer are conscious of the vibrations, but know them by their effect only.

"When the frequency is more than 38,000 vibrations per second, the ear cannot recognize sound; when 400,000,000,000 vibrations have been reached, we perceive the sensation of light, and as the vibrations gradually increase, the eye perceives one color after another until violet is reached with its 75,000,000,000,000 vibrations a second.

Every phenomenon in nature is what it is by virtue of the rate of motion or vibration.

We speak of the sun as "rising" and "setting," though we know that this is simply an appearance of motion. To our senses the earth is apparently standing still. We speak of a bell as ringing, and yet we know that all that the bell can do is to produce vibrations in the air. When these vibrations come at the rate of sixteen a second, they are then frequent enough to set the tympanic membrane in motion from which the vibration is transmitted along a nerve to the brain, where it is registered as "sound." It is possible for the mind to hear vibrations up to the rate of 38,000 a second. When the number increases beyond this, all is silence again. So we know that the sound is not in the bell, but is in our own mind.

We speak and even think of the Sun as "giving light." Yet we know that it is simply giving forth energy that produces vibrations in the ether at the rate of four hundred trillion a second, causing what are termed light waves, so that what is called light is simply a mode of motion, and the only light that there is, is the sensation produced in the mind by the motion of these waves. When the number of vibrations increases, the light changes in color, each change being caused by shorter and more rapid vibrations; so that although we speak of the rose as being red, the grass as being green, or the sky as being blue, we know that these colors exist only in our minds, and are the sensation experienced by us as the result of a particular rate of vibration. When vibrations are reduced below four hundred trillion a second, they no longer affect us as light, but we experience the sensation of heat.

How To Read The Human Aura And Create An Intelligent Life Form

Scientific observations have shown that the Earth's temperature declines one degree at the height of 100 feet above the Earth's surface, and that there is a difference in temperature corresponding to each 100 feet; and it has been assumed that beyond a certain radius from the Earth's surface—beyond its atmosphere—dense darkness, with corresponding density of cold, reigns supreme.

The French aviator Jean Callizo, who holds the world's record and attained a height of 40,820 feet, said that the last observation which he could make of his thermometer showed a temperature of 58 degrees below zero, but soon the mercury sunk out of sight below the armature, so that he had no means of knowing how cold it became. Notwithstanding the fact that he wore four pairs of gloves—paper, silk, wool, and leather—his fingers became numb.

If the Sun gave light and heat as many suppose, all space would be flooded with light; there would be no night because the entire orbit in which the Earth moves would be filled with light. No star would be visible because the stars are not visible in the light.

The Sun is 93,000,000 miles away from the Earth. It is a great dynamo 866,000 miles in diameter. It sends electromagnetic currents throughout all solar space, which is something like six billion miles from end to end. It turns on its axis like the planets, and is but one of thousands of similar systems of suns and planets, many of them much greater in extent, all of them moving forward in space and all revolving around one common center.

It is clear, then, that instead of giving light and heat, the Sun gives forth electrical energy only. This energy contacts with the atmosphere of the Earth in the form of rays. As the Earth is revolving at the incredible speed of more than a thousand miles an hour at its circumference, the atmosphere coming in contact with the electric rays of the Sun becomes incandescent, causing the sensations of light and heat.

As the Earth revolves at a constantly decreasing speed as we reach the poles, the friction becomes less and less and so we find less light and less heat as the poles are reached, until at the poles there is little light and no heat. What we know as light, therefore, appears only in the atmosphere, and not outside of it, and in that part of the atmosphere only which is turned toward the Sun.

As we ascend from the Earth, the atmosphere becomes more rare, and there is consequently less friction, and therefore less light and less heat.

As the direct rays of electrical energy from the Sun reach only that pan of the Earth that is turned toward the Sun, light appears on that side only. The other side of the Earth, being turned away from the Sun, there is no friction and consequently no light, but as the Earth turns upon its axis, the atmosphere gradually comes into direct contact with the electrical rays from the Sun and light appears.

The more direct the rays are that strike the Earth, the stronger the friction, the brighter the light, and the greater the heat. This solar phenomenon we call morning, noon, and night.

A man sees because of the activity of the optic nerve, by which light vibrations are communicated to the sensorium, where they produce the images of things. This sensorium is the corresponding center in the brain that is energized by a force connected with the luminiferous ether; hence, the act of seeing is identical with the making of the image of the thing seen. In fact, what we see is the image and not the object.

How To Read The Human Aura And Create An Intelligent Life Form

A reflex is an involuntary act. When light, which is radiant energy, strikes the eye, the pupils contract. These animal reflexes exceed in sensitivity any apparatus yet devised by man.

The retina of the eye is 3,000 times more sensitive than a photographic plate. The sense of smell surpasses in fineness the most impressionable scientific instruments. The lungs antedate the bellows; the heart, the pump; the hand, the lever; and the eye, the photographic camera.

Telephonic and telegraphic apparatus duplicate mimetically what has always been done by the nervous system and always by aid of the same energy.

Scientists make use of the word "ether" in speaking of the substance "in which we live and move and have our being;" which is omnipresent, which interpenetrates everything, and which is the source of all activity. They use the word "ether" because ether implies something which can be measured, and so far as the materialistic school of science is concerned anything that cannot be measured does not exist. But who can measure an electron? And yet the electron is the basis for all material existence, so far as we know at present.

A number of electrons equal to twenty-five million times the population of the Earth must be present in the test tube for a chemist to detect them in a chemical trace. About 125 septillions of atoms are in a cubic inch of lead. And we cannot come anywhere near even seeing an atom through a microscope. Yet the atom is as large as our solar system compared to the electrons of which it is composed.

All atoms are alike in having one positive central sun of energy around which one or more negative charges revolve.

How To Read The Human Aura And Create An Intelligent Life Form

The diameter of an electron is to the diameter of the atom as the diameter of our Earth is to is to the diameter of the orbit in which it moves around the sun. More specifically, it has been determined that an electron is one-eighteen-thousandth of the mass of a hydrogen atom.

It is clear, therefore, that matter is capable of a degree of refinement almost beyond the power of the human mind to conceive. We have not as yet been able to analyze this refinement beyond the electron, and even in getting thus far have had to supplement our physical observation of effect with imagination to cover certain gaps.

From all this, it is plain that the electron is merely an invisible mode of motion—a charge of electrical energy.

Light is then a mode of motion. For it results from the oscillation of the infinitesimal particles that impinge on the cells and awaken the transmuted motion that we call seeing.

The solar fluid is also the medium for the transmission of the potencies organized by the various planets. It holds in solution the basic elements of life. It is the only possible fluid that is sufficiently subtle to carry the delicate vibrations that are constantly being broadcasted over the radio, and which penetrate iron, steel, and every other barrier, and which are not limited by either time or space.

The movement of the planets cause vibrations in the ether. The nature of the vibrations which they send depend upon the particular nature of that planet, as well as its ever changing position in the Zodiac. These emanations are constantly being impressed upon all the worlds of our system by the perfect conductivity of the solar ether.

Throughout the entire Universe, the law of cause and effect is ever at work. This law is supreme; here a cause, there an effect. They can never operate independently. One is supplementary to the other. Nature at all times is endeavoring to establish a perfect equilibrium. This is the law of the Universe and is ever active. Universal harmony is the goal for which all nature strives. The entire cosmos moves under this law. The sun, the moon, the stars are all held in their respective positions because of harmony.

They travel their orbits, they appear at certain times in certain places, and because of the precision of this law, astronomers are able to tell us where various stars will appear in a thousand years. The scientist bases his entire hypothesis on this law of cause and effect. Nowhere is it held in dispute except in the domain of man. Here we find people speaking of luck, chance, accident, and mishap; but is any one of these possible? Is the Universe a unit? If so, and there is law and order in one part, it must extend throughout all parts. This is a scientific deduction.

Ether fills all interplanetary space. This more or less metaphysical substance is the elemental basis of all life and matter.

Matter in motion represents kinetic energy. Ether under strain represents potential energy, and all of the activities of the material universe consist of alterations from one of these forms of energy to the other.

CHAPTER XII
THE MATRIX OF THOUGHT FORMS

WE live in a fathomless sea of plastic mind substance. This substance is ever alive and active. It is sensitive to the highest degree. It takes form according to mental demand. Thought forms the mold or matrix from which the substance expresses. Our ideal is the mold from which our future will emerge.

The Universe is alive. In order to express life, there must be mind; nothing can exist without mind. Everything that exists is some manifestation of this one basic substance from which and by which all things have been created and are continually being recreated. It is man's capacity to think that makes him a creator instead of a creature.

All things are the result of the thought process. Man has accomplished the seemingly impossible because he has refused to consider it impossible. By concentration, men have made the connection between the finite and the Infinite, the limited and the Unlimited, the personal and the Impersonal. The building up of matter from electrons has been an involuntary process of individualizing, intelligent energy.

Men have learned a way to cross the ocean on floating palaces, how to fly in the air, how to transmit thought around the world on sensitized wires, how to cushion the earth with rubber, and thousands of other things just as remarkable, just as startling, and just as incomprehensible to the people of a generation ago.

Men will yet turn to the study of life itself and with the knowledge thus gained will come peace and joy and length of days.

The search for the elixir of life has always been a fascinating study and has taken hold of many minds of Utopian mold. In all times, philosophers have dreamed of the day when man will become the master of matter. Old manuscripts contain many, many receipts that have cost their investors bitter pangs of baffled disillusionment. Thousands of investigators have laid their contributions upon the sacrificial altar for the benefit of mankind.

But not through quarantine or disinfectants or boards of health will man reach the long-sought plane of physical well-being; nor by dieting or tasting or suggesting will the Elixir of Life and the Philosopher's Stone be found.

The Mercury of the Sages and the "hidden manna" are not constituents of health foods.

When man's mind is made perfect, then and then only will the body be able perfectly to express itself.

The physical body is maintained through a process of continuous destruction and reconstruction.

Health is but the equilibrium that nature maintains through the process of creating new tissue and eliminating the old, or waste, tissue.

Hate, envy, criticism, jealousy, competition, selfishness, war, suicide, and murder are the causes that produce acid conditions in the blood, causing changes which result in irritation of the brain cells, the keys upon which the soul plays "divine harmonies" or "fantastic tricks before high heaven" accordingly to the arrangement of chemical molecules in the wondrous laboratory of nature.

Birth and death are constantly taking place in the body. New cells are being created by the process of converting food, water, and air into living tissue.

Every action of the brain, every movement of the muscle, means destruction and consequent death of some of these cells, and the accumulation of these dead, unused, and waste cells is what causes pain, suffering, and disease.

We allow such destructive thoughts as fear, anger, worry, hatred, and jealousy to take possession and these thoughts influence the various functional activities of the body, the brain, the nerves, the heart, the liver, or the kidneys. They in turn refuse to perform their various functions—the constructive processes cease and the destructive processes begin.

Food, water, and air are the three essential elements necessary to sustain life, but there is something still more essential. Every time we breathe, we not only fill our lungs with air, but we fill ourselves with pranic energy, the breath of life replete with every requirement for mind and spirit.

This life giving spirit is far more necessary than air, food, or water. A man can live for forty days without food, for three days without water, and for a few minutes without air; but he cannot live a single second without ether. It is the one prime essential of life, so that the process of breathing furnishes not only food for body building, but food for mind and spirit as well. It is a well-known fact in India, but not so well-known in this country, that in normal, rhythmical breathing, exhalation and inhalation takes place through one nostril at a time—for about one hour through the right nostril and then for a like period through the left nostril.

The breath entering through the right nostril creates positive electromagnetic currents, which pass down the right side of the spine, while the breath entering through the left nostril sends negative electromagnetic currents down the left side of the spine. These currents are transmitted by way of the nerve centers of ganglia of the sympathetic nervous system to all parts of the body.

In the normal, rhythmical breath, exhalation takes about twice the time of inhalation. For instance, if inhalation requires four seconds, exhalation, including a slight natural pause before the new inhalation, requires eight seconds.

The balancing of the electromagnetic energies in the system depend to a large extent upon this rhythmical breathing, hence the importance of deep, unobstructed, rhythmic exhalation and inhalation.

The wise men of India knew that with the breath, they absorbed not only the physical elements of air, but life itself. They taught that this primary force of all forces, from which all energy is derived, ebbs and flows in rhythmical vibration through the created universe. Every living thing is alive by the virtue of partaking of this cosmic breath.

The more positive the demand, the greater the supply. Therefore, while breathing deeply and rhythmically in harmony with the universal breath, we contact the life force from the source of all life in the innermost parts of our being. Without this intimate connection of the individual soul with the great reservoir of life, existence as we know it would be an impossibility.

How To Read The Human Aura And Create An Intelligent Life Form

Freedom does not consist in the disregard of a governing principle, but in conformity to it. The laws of Nature are infinitely just. A violation of just law is not an act of freedom. The laws of Nature are infinitely beneficent. Exception from the operation of a beneficent law is not freedom. Freedom consists in conscious harmonious relation with the Laws of Being. Thus only may desire be satisfied, harmony attained, and happiness secured.

The mighty river is free only while it is confined within its banks. The banks enable it to perform its appointed function and to answer its beneficent purpose to the best advantage. While it is under the restraint of freedom, it gives out its message of harmony and prosperity. If its bed is raised or its volume greatly increased, it leaves its channel and spreads over the country, carrying a message of ruin and desolation. It is no longer free. It has ceased to be a river.

Necessities are demands and demands create action, which result in growth. This process makes for each decade a larger growth. So it is truly said that the last twenty-five years have advanced the world more than any previous century, and the last century has advanced the world more than all the ages of the past.

Notwithstanding all of the different characters, dispositions, and idiosyncrasies of different people, there is a certain definite law that dominates and governs all existence.

Thought is mind in motion, and psychic gravity is to the law of the mind what atomic attraction is to physical science. Mind has its chemistry and constituent powers and these powers are as definite as those of any physical potency.

Creation is the power of mind in which the thought is turned inward and made to impregnate and conceive new thought. It is for this reason that only the enlightened mind can think for itself.

The mind must acquire a certain character of thought, which will enable it to reproduce them itself without any seed from without to impregnate it.

When mind has acquired this nature in accordance with which thoughts are able to reproduce themselves, it is able to spontaneously generate thoughts without outside stimulation.

This is done by conceiving thought in the mind as a result of being impregnated and fecundated by the Universal.

They must not be permitted to go out into space, but on the contrary, must remain within where they will create psychic states corresponding to their natures.

It is this absorption of self-generated thoughts and their conception of corresponding psychic states that is the Principle of Causation.

This is possible owing to the fact that the mental cosmos is perpetually radiated as a unity of mind, and this mind functions in connection with the soul of man as his mind.

It being essence, it is identified with the essence of the cosmos and with the essence of all thing's.

The result is that having attained unto and having become an infinity of thought, the individual is omniscient in mind, omnipotent in will, and omnipresent in soul. The quality of his mind is omniscience and the quality of his soul is omnipresence.

Such a man is possessed with real power in all that he does. He is indeed a Master, the creator of his own destiny, the arbiter of his own fate.

How To Read The Human Aura And Create An Intelligent Life Form

There are many flowers of vari-colored blossoms. Each blossomed stem simply reaches up to the great Sun—the god of vegetable life manifestation—without complaining, without doubt, in all the fullness of plant desire, faith, and expectancy. They demand and attract the richness of color and perfume.

In the future, man too will unshackle the great desire forces of mind and soul and turn them to heaven in righteous demand for the highest gift in the universe, Life.

And life means to live.

Age is a prejudice that has become so firmly anchored in your mind that any casual number of years mentioned evokes a precise image on your brain.

Twenty years, you see a youth or a young girl adorned with all of the juvenile graces.

Thirty years, a young man or young woman in the full development of vital strength and equilibrium, still on the upgrade towards the dazzling heights of maturity.

Forty years, the summit has been reached, the effort made having been maintained by the prospect of the vast horizons to be dominated.

The road traversed is contemplated with pride, but with emotion you already turn towards the abyss whose dizzy curves wind steeply into ever-increasing darkness.

Fifty years, halfway down the slope, which is still illumined by the light from the peaks though already touched by the chill of the abyss. Organism weakened and compelled to submit to numerous abdications.

Sixty years brings you to the entrance of the cold melancholy valleys. Resigned to inexorable destiny, you stand on the threshold of old age. You begin preparations for the long journey that must inevitably be undertaken.

Seventy years, wrinkled and old, endowed with numerous infirmities, you sit in the waiting room for the last journey, considering it miraculous that you are still alive.

If the eightieth year is exceeded, the fact is mentioned as an amazing phenomenon and you are treated with the respect due to antiquities.

Is this parallel correct? Is there any connection between age and age-value? Let it be emphatically stated that the tyranny of the birth certificate can be abolished.

The fact that a year represents one complete revolution of the earth around the sun has nothing in common with the evolution of the human being.

To be so many years old means simply that the circling seasons have been observed so many times, and nothing more. It implies no consideration of the intellectual or physical state. The person who has seen the untiring astronomical phenomenon forty times may be much younger in the real meaning of the word than one who has seen it but thirty times.

The vibratory activities of the planetary universe are governed by a law of periodicity. Everything that lives has periods of birth, growth, and fruitage. These periods are governed by the Septimal Law.

The Law of Sevens governs the days of the week, the phases of the moon, the harmonies of light, heat, electricity, magnetism, and atomic structure. It governs the life of individuals and of nations, and it dominates the activities of the commercial world. We can apply the same law to our own lives and therefore come into an understanding of many experiences that would otherwise appear inexplicable.

Life is growth, and growth is change. Each seven year period takes us into a new cycle. The first seven years is the period of infancy. The next seven is the period of childhood, representing the beginning of individual responsibility.

The next seven represent the period of adolescence. The fourth period marks the attainment of full growth. The fifth period is the constructive period, when men acquire property, possessions, a home and family. The next, from 35-42, is a period of reactions and changes, and this in turn is followed by a period of reconstruction, adjustment, and recuperation, so as to be ready for a new cycle of sevens, beginning with the fiftieth year.

The law of periodicity governs cycles of every description. There are cycles of short periods and cycles of long periods. There are periods when the emotions gain the ascendancy and the whole world is absorbed in religious thought; and there are other periods when science and learning take the ascendancy and the patent office is flooded with new inventions. There are other periods when vice and crime rule with a high hand; periods of strikes and hard times; times of turmoil, confusion, and disaster; and there are periods of reform.

What is the cause of these cycles? Are they arbitrary? Have they no basis or foundation in nature, recurring with almost the regularity of clockwork and without any incentive whatsoever? Or are they perhaps due to Universal Laws and caused by the revolution of the planets in their orbits, having their origin in some principle in nature which man may learn and thus ultimately be able to predict with certainty the recurrence of the same phenomena?

The revolution of the several planets upon their axis constitutes the largest amount of matter in motion with which we are familiar, and consequently is responsible for the largest amount of energy.

The movement of the planets in their various orbits around the Sun brings the largest amount of ether under strain, and thereby brings into existence the largest amount of potential energy with which we are familiar.

All of the activities of the material universe are therefore contingent upon the movements of these several planets.

Let us note the results of these movements. The first result to be noted is the differentiation of the rays of the Sun into seven primary colors—orange, green, violet, yellow, red, indigo, and blue. These seven colors have their correspondences in the seven notes of the musical scale.

We then find that the vibrations of each planet is responsible for the condensation or crystallization of electrons into matter, and so we have gold, silver, mercury, copper, iron, tin, and lead.

By pursuing our inquiry still further, we find that these vibrations are distributed to all parts of our body through the sympathetic nervous system, and that there are seven plexus along the spine for this purpose. We also find that there are seven functions of our body which are controlled—the heart, brain, lungs, veins, gall, liver, and spleen— and finally we find that these vibrations manifest on a still higher plane as spirit, soul, intellect, love, energy, judgment, and memory.

The angle between two planets at some time and place in their established orbits and their angular relation to the Earth causes an influence that is received by those individuals who are receptive or keyed to those particular vibrations.

Under a favorable influence, we find the body relaxed, comfortable, and at ease. This state of being reacts favorably upon the mental condition and we find mental poise, tendency to pleasure, amusement, reaction, happiness, kindness, and love.

If the influence is unfavorable, the body will be tense and irritable with corresponding mental depression, fear, anger, malice, violence, etc., according to the nature of the planets involved. When Saturn contracts the tissues and squeezes out dead elements from the organs, Jupiter does the reverse by expanding and absorbing new elements for the maintenance of growth and development.

The effect of this Jupitarian process on the mind is to make the feelings "Jovial," optimistic, comfortable, carefree, generous, and compassionate; able to look out and beyond self to the needs and happiness of others, with the result that the word and deed bring commendation and support from others—what is done will produce fortunate results.

When Saturn is benignly aspected, the organs and functions affected by vibratory influences of that planet operate in a normal manner, but when Saturn is adversely aspected, its operations in the human body tend to inertia, contractions, restrictions, decay, or dissolution and serious disease results unless the individual is aware of what is necessary in order to counteract the influence.

Herbert Spencer said, "Life is a continual adjustment of internal conditions to external environment," a statement which we all know is absolutely true, just as much as the axiom of the ancient wise men, "As above, so below." Events in the solar system have a corresponding effect in the human system. Much food for thought is furnished by the divisions of the zodiacal circle, taken in connection with the various periods of vital activity that determine the course of life.

The planet uranus makes the circle of the heavens in eighty-four years, which is its "year"; and as this planet is one that has a special influence over man in a spiritual sense, its "month", or passage through a twelfth part of the circle, might well be expected to exercise an influence on the life of man comparable to that exhibited in the physical world by the sun during the various monthly stages of its annual course.

The fact that during each period of seven years a complete change is known to take place in the physical body, as testified to by physiologists, tends to support this theory of a sign ruling over each seven years of life; and certainly the period of eighty-four years may be taken as a life cycle, without necessarily regarding it as marking the limit of normal human life. In this sense, these eighty-four years of life will correspond to the one earth year, or to the circle of the Zodiac.

Let us now consider the division of the Zodiac into four grand quarters resembling Spring, Summer, Autumn, and Winter.

The Spring Quarter corresponds to infancy, childhood, and youth—the irresponsible and educational period from the first to the twenty-first year of life, when the personal is being fitted by service and study for the next important stage. It is the time when fidelity, filial reverence, obedience, and industry are instilled into the growing mind.

How To Read The Human Aura And Create An Intelligent Life Form

The Summer Quarter of life, from 21 to 42, is the practical period of life and is concerned with the life of the householder, in which wealth becomes an object, responsibility grows, and the duties of life become heavier and filled with business activity. It is the period when the social side of the personality is expressed and the lesson of unselfishness is learned. Prosperity comes with the fullness of life which abounds in the Summer portion. The virtues developed are caution, thrift, charity, magnanimity, diligence, and prudence.

This period of life is governed by the sign Leo, in which the life-forces burn at their greatest heat and love for partner and offspring finds its greatest height in the domestic and social world.

The Autumn Quarter of life is one in which the glory of manhood and the fullness of motherhood are turned to wider interest and personal claims are sacrificed for the benefit of those outside the narrow circle of the home. The duties of government and the national welfare are taken up with motives that are less limited and more altruistic in their nature, the desire being to help in the ruling and guiding of those who belong to the nation. The virtues to be acquired are equilibrium, justice, strength, courage, vigor, and generosity.

The concentrating power of this period is denoted by the sign Scorpio, symbol of self-controlled emotions, fixed feelings, and permanent modes of action; the fluidity and changeable sensations of the watery signs being made stable and reliable and fixed.

The next stage of life, the Winter Quarter, is the period in which experience is garnered and the lessons of life are stored, ready for the enriching of the ego. It is the stage in which the review of life brings wisdom and the tender feelings of sympathy to all. The virtues of the last three signs are made manifest as patience and self-sacrifice, service, purity, wisdom, gentleness, and compassion.

The centralizing of the mind in the sign Aquarius brings the climax when the man is complete, and the humanized perfection of manhood culminates in the one whose mind is wholly centered in higher states of consciousness.

This is the plan of the normal evolution of humanity, when the civilized nations have worked through their infantile, spring-like stage. For nations, like individuals, are also evolving, and it is the national good and the national perfection that is to be the outcome of this wisely ordained plan in accordance with the will of the Supreme Ruler of the Universe.

Perhaps it was this national good and national perfection that one of our great men saw when he had the wonderful vision that he so beautifully described.

"A vision of the future arises. I see a world where thrones have crumbled and where kings are dust. The aristocracy of idleness has perished from the earth.

"I see a world without a slave. Man at last is free. Nature's forces have by science been enslaved. Lightening and light, wind and waves, frost and flames, and all the subtle powers of the earth and air are the tireless toilers for the human race.

"I see a world at peace, adorned with every form of art, with music's myriad voices thrilled, while lips are rich with words of love and truth; a world in which no exile sighs, no prisoner mourns; a world in which the gibbet's shadow does not fall; a world where labor reaps its full reward, where work and worth go hand in hand. I see a world without the beggar's outstretched palm, the miser's heartless stony stare, the piteous wail of want, the livid lips of lies, the cruel eyes of scorn.

"I see a race without disease of flesh or brain—shapely and fair, married harmony of form and function—and, as I look, life lengthens, joy deepens, love canopies the earth; and over all, in the great dome, shines the eternal star of faith."

The question that has been asked concerning the creation of Tulpas is "Are Tulpas Alive?" If you create a Tulpa, give it energy and a personality, but then decide later on to "get rid of it," take back its energy and let it fade away...are you committing murder? Let's take a close look at life and how life vibrations permeate the universe.

Life...The Eternal Force

Life is not created—it simply is. All nature is animate with this force we call "Life." The phenomena of life on this physical plane, with which we are chiefly concerned, are produced by the involution of "energy" into "matter," and matter is, itself, an involution of energy.

Living tissue is organized or organic life; dead tissue is unorganized or inorganic matter. When life disappears from an organism, disintegration begins, the process of organization ceases.

Organization requires a high rate of vibration, or short wave length, moving with great intensity. The molecules of which the tissue is composed are in a continuous state of activity. The result is the tissues manifest what we call life.

Life is a rate of vibration, a mode of motion; death is the absence of that vibration. Life is a manifestation of activity. Death is the process of disintegration, the absence of activity.

How To Read The Human Aura And Create An Intelligent Life Form

The universe was built by vibration; that is to say, the specific form that everything has on whether a large or a small scale, is due absolutely to the specific rate of vibration that gave expression to it. The universe, then, both in general and in particular, is the effect of a system of vibration. In other words, the music of the spheres has expressed itself in that form which we denominate the Cosmos.

This vibration expresses intelligence. This is not intelligence as we understand the word, but a cosmic knowledge which is responsible for the growth of finger nails, hair, bones, teeth, and skin, the circulation of blood, and breathing, which proceed whether we are asleep or awake.

Thus, consciousness or intelligence abounds in everything, peculiar only to itself only in that it differs in character to every other thing; for there is but one universal consciousness or intelligence, while there are multitudinous different expressions of it. The rock, the fish, the animal, the human are all recipients of the one universal intelligence. They are only differently formed manifestations of Cosmic substance— differently combined rates of motion or vibration.

Mind is a system of vibration. The brain is the vibrator and thought is the organized effect of each particular vibration when expressed through the requisite combination of cells.

It is not the number of the cells, but their vibratory adaptability which gives range to the thoughts of which the mind is capable.

It is through the Universal Mind that the "seeds of thought" enter the brain of man, so that it conceives thought which becomes a current of energy, centripetal in the mind of man and centrifugal in the Universal Mind.

How To Read The Human Aura And Create An Intelligent Life Form

These seeds of thought have a tendency to germinate, to sprout, and to grow; they thus form that we call ideas.

When a mental picture is formed in the brain, the rate of vibration corresponding to that picture is immediately awakened in the ether. It depends, however, upon whether the Will or Desire principle is acting as to whether that vibration moves inward or outward.

If the Will is used, the vibration moves outward and the principle of force is put into operation. If the Desire nature is awakened, the vibrations move inward and the Law of Attraction is put into operation. In either case, the Law of Causation expresses itself through the embodying of creative principle.

The time is not far distant when man will be able to make the body immune against disease and arrest the ordinary process of old age and physical decay— perpetuate youth even after the body has passed the mark of the centuries.

Immortality, or perpetual life, is the fondest hope, the legitimate goal and just birthright of every human being. But the majority of people of all religions and those of no religious belief at all, seem to think that it is to be attained, if at all, at some future time and on some other plane of existence.

Every human being who is not sick or insane has an innate desire to live as long as possible. If there is an individual person in the world who does not desire to live, it is because he is in some abnormal condition of body or mind or expects to be.

As a matter of fact, the more highly enlightened and developed the individual, the more intense the desire and longing for life, and it is improbable that there would be a natural desire for something that was impossible of attainment.

How To Read The Human Aura And Create An Intelligent Life Form

Prof. Jaques Loeb, formerly of the Department of Psychology at the University of California, said several years ago, "Man will live forever when he has learned to establish the right protoplasmic reaction to the body."

Thomas Edison says, "I have many reasons to believe that the time will come when man will not die."

Five-sevenths of the flesh and blood are water, while the substance of the body consists of albumen, fibrin, cassein, and gelatin; that is, organic substance composed originally of four essential gases—oxygen, nitrogen, hydrogen, and carbonic acid.

Water is a combination of two gases and air is a mixture of three gases. Thus, our bodies are composed of only transformed gases. None of our flesh existed three or four months ago; face, mouth, arms, hair, even the very nails. The entire organism is but a current of molecules, a ceaselessly renewed flame, a stream at which we may look all of our lives and never see the same water again.

These molecules do not touch each other and are continually renewed by means of assimilation—directed, governed, and organized by the immaterial force that animates it.

To this force we may give the name "soul," so writes the great French astronomer, physicist, biologist, and metaphysician Camille Flammarion.

The Bridge of Life, a symbol of physical regenesis, has been exploited in song, drama, and story. Paracelsus, Pythagorus, Lycurgus, Valentin, Wagner, and a long unbroken line of the Illuminati from time immemorial have chanted their epics in unison with this "riddle of the Sphinx," across the scroll of which is written, "Solve me or die."

How To Read The Human Aura And Create An Intelligent Life Form

Mind is then the source of all things, in the sense that the activity of mind is the initial cause of all things coming into being. This is because the primal source of all things is a corresponding thought in the Universal Mind. It is the essence of a thing that constitutes its being and the activity of mind is the cause by which the essence takes form.

An idea is a thought conceived in the mind and this rational form of the thought is the root of form in the sense that this form of thought is the initial formal expression which, acting upon substance, causes it to assume form.

There can be nothing except as there is an idea, or ideal form, engendered in the Mind. Such ideas, acting upon the Universal, engender corresponding forms.

Matter being Cosmic Mind in physical manifestation, we perceive that everything is possessed of intelligence directing its development and manifestation.

All life is from within out. This is something that cannot be reiterated too often. The springs of life are all from within. Everything in the material universe about us, everything the universe has ever known, had its origin first in thought. From this it took its form.

Every castle, every statue, every painting, every piece of mechanism, everything had its birth, its origin, first in the mind of the one who formed it before it received its material expression or embodiment. The very universe in which we live is the result of the thought energies of the Infinite Spirit that is back of all. And if it is true, as we have found, that we in our true selves are in essence the same, and in this sense are one with the life of this Infinite Spirit, do we not then see that in the degree that we come into a vital realization of this stupendous fact, we, through the operation of our interior, spiritual, thought forces, have in like sense creative power?

Everything exists in the unseen before it is manifested or realized in the seen, and in this sense it is true that the unseen things are the real, while the things that are seen are the unreal. The unseen things are cause; the seen things are effect. The unseen things are the eternal; the seen things are the changing, the transient.

The "power of the word" is a literal scientific fact. Through the operation of our thought forces we have creative power. The spoken word is nothing more nor less than the outward expression of the workings of these interior forces. The spoken word is then, in a sense, the means whereby the thought-forces are focused and directed along any particular line; and this concentration, this giving them direction, is necessary before any outward or material manifestation of their power can become evident.

Much is said in regard to "building castles in the air," and one who is given to this building is not always looked upon with favor. But castles in the air are always necessary before we can have castles on the ground, before we can have castles in which to live. The trouble with the one who gives himself to building castles in the air is not that he builds them in the air, but that he does not go farther and actualize in life, in character, in material form, the castles he thus builds. He does part of the work, a very necessary part; but another equally necessary part remains still undone.

There is in connection with the thought-forces what we may term, the drawing power of mind, and the great law operating here is one with that great law of the universe, that like attracts like. We are continually attracting to us from both the seen and the unseen side of life, forces and conditions most akin to those of our own thoughts.

This law is continually operating whether we are conscious of it or not. We are all living, so to speak, in a vast ocean of thought, and the very atmosphere around us is continually filled with the thought forces that are being continually sent or that are continually going out in the form of thought waves. We are all affected, more or less, by these thought forces, either consciously or unconsciously; and in the degree that we are more or less sensitively organized, or in the degree that we are negative and so are open to outside influences, rather than positive, thus determining what influences shall enter into our realm of thought, and hence into our lives.

There are those among us who are much more sensitively organized than others. As an organism their bodies are more finely, more sensitively constructed. These, generally speaking, are people who are always more or less affected by the mentalities of those with whom they come in contact, or in whose company they are. A friend, the editor of one of our great journals, is so sensitively organized that it is impossible for him to attend a gathering, such as a reception, talk and shake hands with a number of people during the course of the evening, without taking on to a greater or less extent their various mental and physical conditions. These affect him to such an extent that he is scarcely himself and in his best condition for work until some two or three days afterward.

Some think it unfortunate for one to be sensitively organized. By no means. It is a good thing, for one may thus be more open and receptive to the higher impulses of the soul within, and to all higher forces and influences from without. It may, however, be unfortunate and extremely inconvenient to be so organized unless one recognize and gain the power of closing himself, of making himself positive to all detrimental or undesirable influences. This power everyone, however sensitively organized he may be, can acquire.

This he can acquire through the mind's action. And, moreover, there is no habit of more value to anyone, be he sensitively or less sensitively organized, than that of occasionally taking and holding himself continually in the attitude of mind -- I close myself, I make myself positive to all things below, and open and receptive to all higher influences, to all things above. By taking this attitude of mind consciously now and then, it soon becomes a habit, and if one is deeply in earnest in regard to it, it puts into operation silent but subtle and powerful influences in effecting the desired results. In this way all lower and undesirable influences from both the seen and the unseen sides of life are closed out, while all higher influences are invited, and in the degree that they are invited will they enter.

The fact of life in whatever form, means the continuance of life, even though the form be changed. Life is the one eternal principle of the universe and so always continues, even though the form of the agency through which it manifests be changed. "In my Father's house are many mansions." And surely, because the individual has dropped, has gone out of the physical body, there is no evidence at all that the life does not go right on the same as before, not commencing, for there is no cessation, but commencing in the other form, exactly where it has left off here; for all life is a continuous evolution, step by step; there one neither skips nor jumps.

CHAPTER XIII
THE FINAL STEP OF VISUALIZATION

To create a Tulpa the final and key step is to learn to visualize successfully. You have to be absolutely certain that you know what it is you want to create...to form its image completely in your mind...and then MAKE IT REAL!

It may sound obvious, but you have to know what you want. Many people don't, and go through life feeling dissatisfied, but much more conscious of what they don't want than of what they actually want.

So now you are going to think about what you really do want, not just in a fuzzy dream-like manner, but in as concrete a way as possible. Ask yourself whether you are willing to accept all the consequences of having what you want. If you want a swimming pool, will you be willing to take care of it, and be vigilant to protect invited and non-invited visitors from the danger of drowning in it? If you want to be a pop singer, are you willing to practice for hours on end, go on grueling tours, sign hundreds of autographs with a smile no matter how tired you are?

Yes, everything has its up side and its down side. To eliminate the negative things in your life, you have to give up any hidden benefits – it could be nothing more than having the right to feel sorry for yourself – and to bring positive things into your life, you have to weigh the possible negative aspects, and say "I still want it."

Next, you have to be clear about why you want it. Write down as many reasons as you can find as to how this will be of benefit to yourself and to those around you.

It's also important to make sure that this is your desire and not someone else's, or what you think others expect of you. Advertisers are masters at creating desires, and making us think that we can't be happy unless we have whatever they are promoting. And more than one graduate has woken up one morning with a diploma in their hands and the realization that they had been following a well-meaning parent's script instead of their own desires.

Sometimes our subconscious desires do not match our conscious ones. This is more difficult to discern, but if you consistently experience failure or feel blocked in areas where you feel that your desire to succeed is strong, there is a great chance that your subconscious mind has a different view of the matter. It may adhere to certain beliefs, perhaps left over from childhood that you have consciously rejected, but that are still there under the surface. In that case, it may be necessary to get professional help or try a belief-changing method such as NLP before proceeding to the visualization. On the other hand, if you manage to persist in the visualization process in spite of a feeling of uneasiness or conflict, this process may help you to change those underlying beliefs and align them with your conscious desires.

You will most probably have a list of several or even many desires after completing the above step. If you are new to the visualization process, it would probably be better to start with something that is not too difficult or that does not take too long to attain. It's like physical exercise – you aren't going to start by running a marathon – you have to train for it.

I would also suggest that you choose just one thing and concentrate on it, or at least don't make your list too long; it will be more difficult to focus on several things.

In our society, we tend to put a lot of emphasis on material things, and our desires are often directed at things that we want to have. And somehow we think that if we can just have "this thing," then we will be able to do something else, and then that will prove that we are this or that.

But in fact, the reverse is closer to the truth. If we can see ourselves as being a certain way, then we can do whatever needs to be done in order to have the thing we desire.

So as you prepare your visualization session, write down what you desire to be first. What kind of person do you need to be for your desire to materialize? Do you want to have a best-selling book? Then you have to see yourself as being a writer. If you want your song to go to the top of the charts, then you have to see yourself as being a singer. Think of all the qualities involved in your desired situation, and write down, "I am organized, I am sensitive, I am shrewd, I am confident," etc.

Then think of the things you are going to do. These activities will flow from the qualities of your being, and will feel much more attainable than if you start from the other end. Write these down too.

Now you can attend to the material aspect, and once again, thinking of what you will have at this point will be a natural outgrowth of what you are and do.

How To Read The Human Aura And Create An Intelligent Life Form

The word "visualization" refers to what we can see, and of course you want to have visual cues. Find pictures of what you want your Tulpa to look like, or draw one yourself. Create a picture in your mind, and describe it in writing. Make it vivid, colorful, attractive and detailed. You can add to this picture during your visualization sessions, but this will serve as a basis. But don't forget the other senses. What will you hear when you attain what you desire? What kind of personality will your Tulpa have? Will it be smart, friendly, loving, fun? Will your Tulpa be something you are familiar with...like a person or favorite animal? Or are you looking at something that has never been seen before...a mystical creature right out of a fairy tale? Your imagination is the limit. If you can think it, you can create it.

Remember, you want to create vivid pictures related to being and doing as well as having. The being part may work better with auditory images, such as imagining yourself saying to someone "I am a writer," or imagining someone saying to you "My goodness, how do you manage to be so organized?"

As mentioned above, it's important that your beliefs be consistent with your desires. In general, there shouldn't be a conflict of values – you want to be sure that you think that what you want is good, both for you and for those around you. So it would be well to write "I desire this for my good and the greater good of all concerned," or whatever wording feels right to you.

You also need to believe that what you desire is actually attainable, at least theoretically, even though you don't yet see how it can come about for you. You will necessarily be stretching your belief limits, because you don't yet have the thing you desire, and you want to be careful not to stretch them too far, or they might snap in your face like a rubber band. This is why the choice of what you want to visualize is so important, especially when you are starting out. Each success will increase your confidence in the process, and you can gradually become more daring.

The highest level of belief is expectancy, that is, you just know that it will happen. It's easier said than done, especially at first. But just doing the process is an expression of your positive expectation. Don't waste time wondering whether you have the right degree of expectation, just imagine that you do. This is visualization, right? So visualize yourself expecting it to happen.

Emotion plays a crucial role in this process. If you really expected something wonderful to happen to you, you would naturally feel good about it. So if your visualization has no emotional content, your subconscious will say "Ho-hum", and the Universe will say "Who are you trying to kid?" Well, they may not actually say that, but would you believe someone who told you about an extraordinary event in a monotone voice? Probably not.

So as you picture the desired result in your mind, as you convince yourself that this is going to happen, let the appropriate emotion come. It might be quiet contentment, or breathless excitement, or just loads of fun. This should be pretty spontaneous, and if you have a lot of trouble with this part, there may be something that needs adjusting in your above preparation. It could be a subconscious conflict, or perhaps your reasons for wanting it are not really very strong.

The emotion of gratitude ought to be present. Gratitude to whom, you may ask? First of all, to the Creator or the Universe, or if you don't believe in them, then gratitude to your subconscious mind and to all those who helped you come this far on your path. Gratitude implies a sense of connection. You probably already have that. If you were some kind of rugged individualist, you probably wouldn't even be reading this book. If you do feel uneasy with the idea of gratitude, then you might have self-esteem issues and doubt whether you really deserve to receive what you desire. As long as this is present, one way or another you (or rather your subconscious mind) will manage to sabotage the process, until you change that belief.

The final emotion is a sense of serenity. This is an outflow of your expectation that positive results will come. How unfortunate for you if stomping your foot and demanding immediate results worked for you when you were a child! They won't work here. They are the contrary to confidence and a spirit of cooperation. You cannot bully the Universe, or your subconscious mind, for that matter.

Many people have found that being in a relaxed state is helpful, perhaps even essential for this process. You could use a relaxation technique, or a hypnosis script, or a binaural beat recording. All of these help the brain produce alpha waves. Choose your technique and prepare it.

The Visualization Process

All of that preparation does seem a bit long, but now that it's all ready, your daily visualizations will go smoothly.

1 – Relax

Use the method you have prepared. If you're using binaural beats, you can keep listening to them during the rest of the process.

2 – Visualize

Using the pictures, images, and written notes that you have gathered, imagine the thing that you desire as if it was already realized in the here and now, in the order of being, then doing, then having. Enjoy the positive feelings. Note your physical sensations related to your feelings. Remember that these positive feelings come from anticipation of something that is on its way to your reality, not just idle dreaming. The physical support of pictures and written notes will help keep you from getting distracted, but if you do find your attention wandering, just bring it back gently.

Do it for about ten to fifteen minutes once or twice a day. One ideal time is just after you wake up, because you are likely to be in an alpha state then. Another good time is just before you go to bed. Here too, the alpha state will be easier to attain. Moreover, you can reinforce the effect by instructing your subconscious mind to continue working on this question while you are sleeping.

3 – Let go

Yes, when you've finished your visualization, just let go of the whole thing and turn you attention to your daily activities. If you have a spirit of serenity, as discussed earlier, this will not be difficult.

4 – Take some kind of action

You can do this at any time of the day. Do something concrete related to your desire. Do an Internet search on the country you want to visit, clean out your clothes closet to make room for the new clothes you will be able to buy, start taking singing lessons to prepare for your singing career. You do not need to spend money at this time, and stretching your budget would be unreasonable and putting the cart before the horse. But doing something, even a symbolic gesture, will show that you mean business.

If you have negative thoughts at any time, shoo them out the door. Any negative thoughts can reflect on the personality of your Tulpa. It's understandable to have negative thoughts, just as it's understandable that your cat will take advantage of a lack of vigilance on your part, but you're not going to let either of them get the upper hand.

However, if this process causes a great deal of anxiety, or if you find yourself forgetting to do it altogether, there is likely to be a subconscious conflict that has not been resolved, and you would do well to re-examine your beliefs, with outside help if necessary.

For those who are still having problems with their Tulpa visualization, an online writer who goes by the name of Shockk has put together an excellent and simple visualization guide intended to help people who have trouble visualizing their Tulpa, or who have trouble visualizing anything.

"Begin by visualizing a canvas in your mind. The canvas can be any color but if you really can't decide, use white. At this point, your Tulpa should use some sort of pen to draw the number 0 on the current page of the canvas. The pen can be any color but you should be able to see it on the canvas's color (so don't pick white if the canvas is white).

"Next, relax your body and mind slightly and become aware of your breathing. Take a minute or so to get to a level where you feel sufficiently relaxed. This will help you stay focused while doing the exercise.

"Now, ask your Tulpa to turn to the next page on the canvas, and then write the number 1. You should try and focus on them in your visualization and watch their movements as they turn the page (or magic the canvas blank if they so desire). Then ask them to move on to the next number.

"Continue this all the way to the number 100 without getting distracted! If you lose focus, your Tulpa should throw the canvas away and get a new one. To throw in a twist, your tulpa is also allowed to make you start again if they think you took too long to ask them for the next number, or if you didn't try to visualize them during a number!

"You might not be able to reach 100 on the first try, but don't worry. Each time you try this, you'll improve your visualization skills more and more and as a bonus, communication between you and your Tulpa will also improve! If you keep practicing, you'll be able to reach 100 before long. Practice makes perfect!

"Ideally, you should do this exercise at least once a day if you want to improve your visualization skills more than a little. As you do it, remember to have fun and feel free to chat with your Tulpa during it (and for the Tulpa: feel free to chat to your host if you want to give them more to focus on!)."

There you go. Good luck and enjoy your Tulpa.

Drop us a line for your FREE Catalog!

Send your name and mailing address to:

Inner Light/Global Communications
P.O. Box 753
New Brunswick, NJ 08903

Email: mrufo8@hotmail.com

www.conspiracyjournal.com

WE ACCEPT CHECKS, MONEY ORDERS, CREDIT CARDS WESTERN UNION, PAYPAL

MARIA D'ANDREA TELLS YOU HOW TO SEE THE FUTURE AND CAST SPELLS WITH AN ORDINARY DECK OF PLAYING CARDS

NOW YOU CAN GO BEYOND CARD GAMES OF MERE "CHANCE" AND INTO THE INFINITE!

The origin of playing cards is shrouded in the mists of time. Some historians trace them to the ancient Egyptians, others to the Chinese or medieval Italy, still others to the Romany gypsies seen so often in pop culture portrayals of fortune tellers. Wherever they come from, an ordinary deck of 52 playing cards are not mere "playthings" but are instead a mystical link to the great unknown. Anyone can master their use with diligent practice – and being born with supernatural powers is not required!

Learn how individual cards are like living entities with personalities and traits all their own. The king of clubs, for example, is humane, upright and affectionate, while the king of diamonds is continually fuming in his stubborn, vengeful wrath. The cards form a cast of characters enacting a drama that can give insight into your future and alert you to dangers you never previously imagined.

But one doesn't have to passively accept the fortune meted out by the seemingly "random" way the cards fall. Read Maria D'Andrea's spells involving the use of playing cards. She explains how the careful laying out of ordinary cards, when combined with the use of candles, incense and the recitation of ritual words, can make the "higher powers" do your bidding. You are in control of your future with Maria's methods and are not subject to the whims of unseen forces working through artful pieces of cardboard. This is a golden opportunity to gaze and control the future – from a perspective of self-determination – that you can't afford to miss!

Order your copy of SIMPLE SPELLS WITH PLAYING CARDS for only $22.00 + $5 S/H

* * * * *

ALSO AVAILABLE
GYPSY WITCH FORTUNE TELLING PLAYING CARDS – $12.00

Perfect for teaching yourself or others to use regular playing cards in your divination, the Gypsy Witch Fortune Telling Playing Cards include small descriptive meaning on each card's face. This has been a popular deck for decades. Says one user: "Some people say these cards are just for fun, but these cards are not a game. I've had done readings on myself and others, they've turned out to be at least 90% accurate, both good and bad."

IF YOU WANT TO LEARN MORE ABOUT THE OCCULT THESE BOOKS BY MARIA D' ANDREA WILL BE MOST HELPFUL TO YOU! EACH BOOK $22.00 OR ALL EIGHT TITLES THIS PAGE FOR $139.00 + $15.00 S/H

( ) SECRET MAGICAL ELIXIRS OF LIFE
( ) HEAVEN SENT MONEY SPELLS
( ) SECRET OCCULT GALLERY AND SPELL CASTING FORMULARY
( ) YOUR PERSONAL MEGA POWER SPELLS
( ) HOW TO ELIMINATE ANXIETY AND STRESS THROUGH THE OCCULT
( ) MYSTICAL AND MAGICAL BEASTS AND BEINGS
( ) OCCULT GRIMORIE AND MAGICAL FORMULARY

ALSO AVAILABLE — 10 Thirty Minute Workshops by Maria on DVD - $80

ORDER NOW FROM: TIMOTHY G. BECKLEY, BOX 753, NEW BRUNSWICK, NJ 08903

WATCH AND SUBSCRIBE TO OUR FREE YOUTUBE CHANNEL—MR UFOS SECRET FILES

Updated Edition!
SECRETS OF THE REAL DOCTOR FRANKENSTEIN
Mad Scientist
Andrew Crosse— Monster Maker

Did he create the building blocks of life in his laboratory? Or was he delusional? Or perhaps even a total fraud? His contemporaries in the scientific community were puzzled by the very nature of his experiments. And while the eye does not deceive, they were unable to duplicate his findings and reproduce under controlled conditions the striking life forms that were plainly visible and clearly moving around Crosse's laboratory table.

To the farmers living in the area surrounding Crosse's palatial Fyne Court, he quickly became recognized as a heretic dabbling in dark areas that led him to be on the receiving end of a significant number of irate letters from God-fearing folk who summarily and loudly accused him of blasphemy, or even trying to replace their God as the ultimate creator.

The contentions of the nearby country folk were only compounded by Andrew Crosse's ability to seemingly capture bolts of lightning and direct them through a mile long coil of copper wire that was suspended from poles and trees all around his estate. Events reached a boiling point when Crosse began to receive anonymous death threats. There were those who firmly blamed him for a failure in the year's wheat-crop; and there was even a demand that an exorcism of the whole area be undertaken in the surrounding green hills. It is said that the author of Frankenstein, Mary Shelly, got her inspiration from Crosse's "demented" laboratory experiments.

Order: Secrets of Dr Frankenstein – $22.00
Large Format – 350 Pages—ISBN: 16061111906
Timothy Green Beckley Box 753 · New Brunswick, NJ 08903

SPECIAL – THREE BOOKS—*The Bell Witch, Mad Mollie* and *Secrets Of The Real Doctor Frankenstein*— 49.00 + $5.00 S/H
(SEE THE NEXT PAGE)

DARE YOU FIND THE TRUTH ABOUT?..
America's Strange And Supernatural History:
Includes: Prophecies Of The Presidents

No one would likely dispute the fact that times are stranger in America than ever, and indications are things are getting weirder with each passing day. But a look at our hidden – SECRET – history alerts us to the startling fact that our country has been steeped in "high strangeness" since the Declaration of Independence was signed. It is apparent that our proud nation owes a great "debt of gratitude" to the mysterious, the macabre, the downright bizarre unseen realm of the occult.

** – Did the Lemurians, a Pacific Ocean race similar to the fabled Atlanteans to the east, erect the mysterious walls found in the eastern part of the San Francisco Bay area? **Writer Olav Phillips** explores the enigma first hand.

** – **Sean Casteel** provides an overview of historical incidents of cannibalism, stories that go back as far as "The Starving Time" of the Jamestown colony in 1609.

** – **William Michael Mott** offers up some of the UFO and creature sightings he has collected from the state of Mississippi – going way back.

** – Publisher/writer **Timothy Green Beckley** and his friend **Circe** returned to Sleepy Hollow, New York – of "Headless Horseman" fame – and discovered that paranormal activity is still rampant there.

** —Author **Tim Swartz** would like suitable explanations for all the supernatural mysteries of his native Indiana, including lake monsters, Bigfoot sightings, anomalous big cats, UFOs and more. As well as the the "demon gasser" of Mattoon, Illinois who did his best to contaminate several small communities.

In a Bonus Section: "The Spiritual Destiny of America" - The future of America as seen through the eyes of prophecy and the occult is revealed. You can feel the chills already, eh?

Order: AMERICA'S STRANGE AND SUPERNATURAL HISTORY
for just $20.00 + $5 S/H
and get ready to kick those chills up a notch or two.

OUR MOTTO: "AND THE TRUTH SHALL SET YOU FREE!" BE AWARE! READ MORE!

NIKOLA TESLA'S "MIRACLE" ENERGY PLATES

3 SIZES NOW AVAILABLE!

Though not approved by the FDA or AMA, regular users say the plates function as Transceivers, creating a field of energy around themselves. This energy is very beneficial to ALL living things.

☐ **LARGE PLATE** - Approx 12x12. Best for using under mattress, chair or in refrigerator to keep food fresh. Ease muscle tension, anxiety. — $75 or 3 for $200 + $8 S/H

☐ **SMALL PLATE**. - Approx. 4x2. For litter box to keep fresh. Flowers live longer. Under car seat. — $25 each. 3 for $68 + $5 S/H

☐ **LARGE DISC** - Create necklace, earings for yourself. Use as animal collar. Carry in wallet or shoe. — $17.50 each. 3 for $40 + $5 S/H

SPECIAL - ONE OF EACH SIZE $112 +$8 S/H FREE *"HOW TO USE TESLA PLATES"* DVD WITH MARIA D' ANDREA AND PRINTED REPORT ON MANY BENEFITS.

Timothy Green Beckley
Box 753
New Brunswick, NJ 08903
MRUFO8@hotmail.com

Free DVD and report with all orders.

AND THE TRUTH SHALL SET YOU FREE!

Our books, products and services are for experimental purposes. They are not endorsed by the AMA, FDA or any other federal or local agency. We offer our merchandise on a non-returnable basis to those who seek the truth about matters neglected by the "Establishment." We appreciate your patronage and hope you will tell all your like-minded friends about our publications.
—Timothy G. Beckley
www.conspiracyjournal.com/
www.teslasecretlab.com

Researchers Promote Use Of The Crystal Power Rod As A Modern Day WISH MACHINE

THE CRYSTAL POWER ROD AS A "WISH MACHINE"

Also Known Widely As The COSMIC GENERATOR this device is believed to have originated in Atlantis and supposedly operates with energy generated by the operator's mind, amplified by emotions, feelings, desires. Once amplified, these "wishes" can be projected over vast distances to influence others.

WISH MACHINES – MIND MACHINES
They come in various forms and are known as Radionics, Ociloclasts, or Hieronymous Machines, Detector Rods, Symbolic Machines or, put most simply, Black Boxes regardless of their appearance.

SUPER SECRET DOSSIER INCLUDED WITH YOUR POWER ROD
Your Crystal Power Rod (may vary slightly from illustration) and Mind Machine Study Guide is sold as a unit for $85.00 + $5.00 S/H and is obtainable only from:

Timothy Beckley · Box 753
New Brunswick, NJ 08903

THE WONDER BOOK OF ALL AGES!
SPECIAL RAY PALMER EDITION!
1250 Pages, 2 Volumes.
Illustrations.
Most Complete Edition

A New Cosmology! Delivered thru spirit intervention in 1870 in upstate NY to a practicing dentist. Details the sacred history of earth for the past 24,000 years beginning with submersion of Pan in the Pacific.

Tells about Einstein's theories. War in space. Who manages the earth. The glory of gods and goddesses. The truth about flying saucers.

A profound work deserving of serious attention.

Our special price $85.00 + $14 S/H.
Mailed directly from the printer
due to weight of seven pounds.
Add $14 for S/H for this item only.

Timothy Beckley · Box 753
New Brunswick, NJ 08903

www.ingramcontent.com/pod-product-compliance
Lightning Source LLC
Chambersburg PA
CBHW070541170426
43200CB00011B/2503